My Flight to Freedom

Written By Ilir Nina

Acknowledgments

To my family, friends, and everyone who supported me on this journey—thank you from the bottom of my heart.

First and foremost, I want to acknowledge my family. To my wife, **Anile**, thank you for your unwavering support and encouragement throughout the years. You believed in me when I struggled to find the words and continually pushed me to sit down and share my story. Your patience and faith in this project have been my greatest strength, and for that, I am forever grateful.

To my children, **Yllka and Aries Nina**, thank you for being part of this story and for inspiring me to finally put it into words. Watching your genuine interest and seeing how deeply my journey resonated with you gave me the courage to continue. Your eagerness to read fragments of the manuscript as I worked on it meant more to me than I can express. You fueled my determination to finish and bring this story to life.

I also want to extend my heartfelt gratitude to **Ann Hart**, who became like a mother to me during my early days in America. Ann, your kindness and unwavering support in Boise, Idaho, when I was finding my footing in a new world, were truly life changing. You encouraged me to document my experiences even as I was busy pursuing my undergraduate studies. Without your guidance and belief in me, this story might have remained untold.

To Professor **Linda Kozar**, my English 101 instructor at Boise State University, thank you for showing me that my story mattered. Your thoughtful feedback and belief in the significance of my experiences planted the seed that has now grown into this book. Even though it took over 30 years to complete, your words of encouragement never left my heart.

A special thank you to **Andrew, my daughter's boyfriend,** and **Kailen, my son's Fiancé,** for their steadfast support and encouragement to see this book through to the end. Your belief in me kept me focused and motivated, even during moments of doubt

Finally, I want to thank everyone from my siblings who played a role, big or small, in helping me tell this story. This book is not just my journey, it is a testament to the power of resilience, hope, and the kindness of those who stand by us during life's most challenging times. It belongs as much to you as it does to me.

With all my gratitude,
Ilir Nina

About the Author

Ilir Nina is a refugee-turned-entrepreneur whose extraordinary journey began with a daring escape from Albania's oppressive communist regime at a young age. After enduring the challenges of displacement and arriving in the United States, he faced a new set of battles: overcoming alcoholism, drugs, and the emotional and mental complexities of adapting to a new life.

Today, Ilir is a highly successful Certified Public Accountant (CPA) in Boise, Idaho. He owns and operates a thriving firm that employs a growing team of professionals, with ambitions to expand nationally in the field of tax resolution. Despite his accomplishments, Ilir's path was far from easy. He changed careers and educational directions multiple times and faced significant hurdles along the way, including the daunting challenge of passing the CPA exam. It took him seventeen attempts to succeed, a testament to his determination and perseverance in the face of obstacles such as language barriers and personal struggles.

Ilir wrote this book to inspire others, planting the seed of hope for anyone who feels defeated by life's challenges, whether external or self-inflicted. His story is a powerful reminder that failure is not the end, but a steppingstone to success. It reflects his deep belief that no matter where you come from or what you've been through, there is always hope for a brighter future if you keep fighting forward.

Through his work and his story, Ilir shares the message that life is worth living and that America offers unmatched opportunities for anyone willing to embrace them. With resilience, gratitude, and unwavering faith in the possibilities of this country, Ilir stands as a shining example of what it means to turn adversity into triumph.

Ilir Nina, CPA, EA, MSAT

Epigraph
"Freedom is nothing else but a chance to be better."
— Albert Camus

4

Introduction

Seated in the plush leather chair within the confines of my home office, located in the affluent neighborhood of Eagle, Idaho, my gaze fixates on the scenery beyond the window. In an unexpected turn, my thoughts drift back to a somber and painful chapter from my past.

The haunting strains of an old Serbian song, a melody engraved in my memory from years gone by, permeate the room. While Serbian folk music typically acts as a balm for my emotions, this specific composition acts as a catalyst, unleashing a torrent of memories. Despite the pain embedded in my history, a peculiar longing arises within me, a yearning to revisit that tumultuous era. Tears well up in my eyes as I reflect on those bygone days.

Turning my attention back to the window, I observe my neighbor Larry, an aficionado of motorcycles and proud owner of numerous antique cars and bikes. He maneuvers his latest acquisition near the playground to the west of my residence, testing its capabilities. The street adjacent to mine, where Larry resides, stretches westward before culminating in a circular turnaround just three houses down from mine. The properties in this contemporary Eagle subdivision boast expansive lots and luxurious homes, with prices starting at a staggering one million dollars.

The ambient light filters through the cloudy sky, creating a serene atmosphere outside. As my gaze lingers, I notice Larry's garbage can flanked by five brown bags filled with leaves, patiently awaiting the arrival of the garbage collector. Here I am, living the quintessential American dream—a beautiful family, a thriving business, and an opulent home—yet an overwhelming sadness persists. Gratitude for the bestowed material success courses through me, a recognition of the blessings granted by God and the United States of America. Nevertheless, the specter of the past refuses to dissipate.

On one hand, I am thankful for having endured and survived. Yet, on the other, the echoes of the past continue to cast a shadow over my present. On the flip side, a surge of rage engulfs me when the details of the past flood my consciousness, overwhelming me with emotion.

Chapter 1

Earliest Memories

My journey began as an escapee from a communist regime, a story that traces back to my unconventional arrival into the world. I was born in Klenje, a small mountain village in Albania, on July 3, 1969, arriving prematurely at just seven months. My early entrance was a struggle for survival, as the odds were not in my favor in a time and place where modern medical advancements were scarce. The tiny hospital where I was supposed to be born was ill-equipped for preterm infants, and my parents relied heavily on the resourcefulness of village traditions and sheer luck to keep me alive.

I was the fifth son of Dule and Aishe Nina, a family of modest means whose lives revolved around hard work and survival under the oppressive grip of a communist regime. My premature birth became a defining characteristic, often remembered with a mix of humor and tenderness by my family. My Aunt Lirije, my mother's sister, christened me Ilir and often teased, with a fond smile, that I was "short a brick." It was her way of acknowledging the physical frailty I carried in my early years, a constant reminder of the precarious start to my life.

Growing up, the story of my premature birth became a family legend, told and retold around the fire on cold Albanian nights. My mother, Aishe, would recount the challenges of feeding and caring for a baby so small and fragile. "We wrapped you in layers of cloth and kept you close to the fire," she'd say. "There was no incubator, no doctors to guide us, just prayers and the belief that you were meant to survive."

The village of Klenje itself seemed to echo the adversity I faced as a child. My arrival into this world was far from ordinary. The day I was born, my mother had visited the local doctor, who confidently told her she had weeks to go before labor. Yet, that very evening, I was born—right in the confines of our home, in an old-fashioned bathroom typical of the Albanian villages. It was a cramped space with no modern amenities, just a rudimentary pit toilet and a pervasive smell that lingered in the air.

Over the years, my mother would recount this story with a mix of amusement and exasperation. I often teased her, joking, "What if I had been flushed away?" She'd laugh and remind me that, in those days, there was no flushing. But the thought often left me unsettled. The image of a newborn teetering on the edge of such precarious conditions filled me with an odd blend of humor and anxiety. It was a stark reminder of the harsh realities of life in those times.

These bathrooms were emblematic of the struggles my family and others in our village faced daily. There was no running water, no sanitation, and the constant smell was something you learned to endure. For a premature baby born in such circumstances, survival itself was nothing short of a miracle. My mother's resourcefulness and determination, coupled with the basic care provided by the local midwives, were all that stood between me and the countless risks of infection or illness.

I would often imagine the scene: my mother, caught off guard, delivering me alone in that unwelcoming space. It spoke volumes about the resilience required to live under such conditions. Yet, despite the odds, my family persevered, and so did I. My arrival, however unconventional, marked the beginning of a life filled with struggles, survival, and an enduring will to overcome whatever came my way.

The harshness of life in Klenje shaped my earliest memories. Winters were brutal, with snow covering the ground from September to May, and the biting cold seemed relentless. Our home, though modest, was filled with the warmth of family, and the stories of my birth became a testament to that strength. They were not just tales of survival but a reminder of the love and grit that defined my family in the face of adversity.

As I recline in my leather chair, closing my eyes transports me back to my early childhood at the earliest I can remember. In this earliest recollection, I find myself tugging against a rope tethered to a massive spike in the corner of the room, fastened around my waist by my grandmother. The struggle is fueled by a desire to join my older brother and his friends playing outside. My grandmother, acting as my guardian, would routinely fasten me to the sizable nail like a dog on a leash when she had chores to attend to. Pulling with all my might, I would scream at the top of my lungs, desperately attempting to break free from the bonds of captivity. Despite my relentless efforts, I would succumb to exhaustion, falling asleep in defeat. The memory of that struggle against confinement persists within me, as vivid today as it was yesterday.

I recollect the overwhelming sense of sadness and self-pity that consumed me at such an early age, a feeling of defeat that lingers in my memories. Situated in east-central Albania on the Macedonian border, Klenje is a village nestled in rugged and mountainous terrain, enduring harsh winters with snowfall from September to often as late as May. The entire village clings to the slope of a mountain, particularly the eastern region, perched on the immediate high ground of Golemo Mountain. Dense Silver Panje trees dominate the landscape, providing a stark backdrop to the challenging conditions of my formative years.

About two kilometers on the eastern side, a dense canopy of trees dominated the landscape, while on the northeast side of the same mountain, majestic Oak trees stood tall and beautiful. Moving towards the northwestern side of the village, beyond small peaks, lay the renowned Kenja field, or "Klencko pole" in the native Bulgarian language, celebrated for cultivating the most famous potatoes in Albania.

Descending on the southern side, the slope led to the village of Borove, where the main creek flowed, and a few miles further downstream, the climate became milder. Flowing southeast from Golemo Mountain, the creek marked the emergence of pine trees as the weather grew warmer. However, the high banks of the creek harbored perilous outcroppings, leading to tragic accidents and fatalities. Many villagers met their end by accidentally falling into the creek, resembling a descent from rugged canyon walls with only a small stream at the bottom. On the western side, the mountain of Osoi loomed, adorned with colossal rocks that could be rolled down to startle those traversing the road at its base.

Members of the communist party utilized the mountain of Osoi for propaganda, inscribing slogans about the party and its leader, Enver Hoxha. Annually, the community was compelled to light a massive fire at the mountain's summit and carry torches in support of the government. Slogans like "Long live our Leader Enver Hoxha," "Down with Imperialist America," and "Praise the communist party" adorned the landscape.

Nestled in the heart of the village, my house occupied a central location. The village comprised two blocks on the northeast and southwest sides, known as "Dimoi" and "Zunoi," respectively. Three cemeteries were present, each side having one for Muslims, while the third, exclusively for Serbian Orthodox Christians, lay above the village's midpoint and just uphill from my house. As I remember on my childhood, I remember how well we knew the villagers—it was almost like a game we played within our family. We had a unique way of guessing the composition of other families in the village, referring to males as "roosters" and females as "chickens." It became a playful challenge to see who could accurately determine the number of people in a family and break it down by gender. One person would start by posing a question: "Do you know how many roosters and chickens are in this family of three and five?" The rest of us would guess, trying to figure out how many boys, girls, and adults made up that household. It was a test of observation and memory, as we relied on snippets of information gleaned from daily interactions and the stories passed around the village.

The smartest among us—usually someone with a keen memory for details—would win by piecing together the right answer. It wasn't just a game of numbers but a way to connect with and understand the people around us.

It reflected the close-knit nature of our community, where everyone's story was known, shared, and sometimes turned into lighthearted fun. Looking back, those moments weren't just about guessing; they were about bonding and cherishing the small, simple joys of village life.

The communist regime imposed strict prohibitions on religious practices, with stories circulating about individuals being jailed for seven to ten years merely for praying. Despite its modest size of around 100 households, the village fostered a unique closeness in the community where everyone knew each other intimately.

The communist government maintained a tight grip on the villagers, suppressing any dissenting comments against the government, as the walls seemingly had ears. The main road, where buses reached the village, ran through the center, linking the community to the outside world. My village exuded a dynamic atmosphere, serving as a central hub where buses converged. To the south lay the city of Elbasan, and northeast, the city of Peshkopi—an area where I often spent time with childhood friends. Despite the constraints of the communist government dictating our actions and words, we managed to find joy in our childhood escapades. Soccer was our passion, and we crafted makeshift balls from old clothing like shirts and pants.

In my village, a two-tiered system governed sports, all administered by the school. The privilege of enjoying sports equipment like soccer balls and skis was reserved for those connected to the Communist Party. Even if a child displayed talent, the coach's decisions predetermined who would receive such equipment. For my family, life was challenging. My father's struggles with alcoholism left him with little influence in the village, and we were often hungry. My mother toiled all day for a mere thirty Albanian leks, barely enough for a pack of cigarettes at that time.

Winters were harsh, with snow persisting from its early onset until May. I endured freezing toes each winter, harboring a strong dislike for the bitter cold. Our house, comprised of three bedrooms and a hallway, faced westward, with two rooms on the sides and one in the center. The central room served as our kitchen, warmed by a wood stove. However, the sleeping quarters, especially my room to the east, remained frigid. Year after year, my wish persisted—to be somewhere beyond Albania, in isolated rooms with better conditions.

From an early age, I recognized the communists as an oppressive and perilous regime. People faced imprisonment merely for voicing grievances about the bread. Despite this awareness, I, as a child, was a troublemaker who challenged the government and the school officials whenever an opportunity arose. My rebellious acts mostly involved criticizing the government. As I entered my teenage years at fifteen, hunger drove me to engage in various illicit activities, seeking to take from the government's resources. The government owned livestock, wheat, and even the potatoes, despite our village being a major exporter of potatoes in Albania. Determined to address our hunger, I began stealing hay, wheat, and potatoes from the government under the cover of darkness.

To evade the guards, I would lie on top of my grandmother's grave at night, drawing strength from the belief that her love for me would shield me. It felt like the only sanctuary until the danger passed. My nighttime escapades gradually grew bolder, and I drew the attention of authorities who began to suspect I was involved in rebellious activities.

In a moment of open defiance, I inscribed the letters "WC" next to Enver Hoxha's name on the eighth Congress book letters stood for "water closet," a common term for a toilet, and were meant as a mocking insult to the oppressive regime.

I went further by stealing an entire goat from the government. It was an act of both rebellion and survival, as I brought the goat home to provide much-needed meat for my family.

nutrition for my family.

One fateful year, trouble at school led to a severe punishment—I was expelled forever under the communist regime. Those days were lonely, filled with tears and a sense of loss. My family believed I was a lost cause, and it felt like my life had come to an abrupt end. As an additional punishment, the school and the Communist Party sentenced me to hard labor in a rock quarry, enduring the toughest physical labor of my life. The days were grueling, with insufficient connections to family and limited food. Working twelve hours a day, seven days a week, I despised every moment and often cried at night, feeling sorry for myself. Faced with aggression from others, particularly older kids, I developed a survival mechanism, using intimidation to protect myself.

Amidst the insensitivity and hardships of communism, the realization that I could never return to school spurred me to plan my escape. I yearned to go beyond the mountains, although I knew nothing about life outside the communist regime. Despite the uncertainty, the decision to escape Albania became a pivotal moment, marking a belief that it was the best thing I could ever do.

Chapter 2

The First Attempt of an Escape

In May 1988, fueled by alcohol consumed during the Albanian Veteran's Day celebrations, I made a bold attempt to break free. After traveling an hour into the mountains and crossing the border, a sudden pang of guilt for leaving my family behind led me to return that same evening. I vaguely remember the muddy, rainy night and the internal struggle of crossing and then retracing my steps.

That evening was drenched in relentless rain, the kind that soaks through every layer and leaves the air heavy with dampness. On my way back home, tipsy from drinking, I stumbled and lost my footing on the slippery mountain slopes. Before I knew it, I was rolling down the muddy hillside, my clothes caked in wet earth by the time I stopped. Exhausted and disoriented, I eventually made it home.

When I arrived, I found my mother still awake, even though it was late into the night. She was sitting near the wood stove, her head resting on its lukewarm surface, its fire long since burned out. Her shoulders shook with quiet sobs, and the sight of her like that made my heart sink. I approached her cautiously and asked, "What's wrong?" She lifted her tear-streaked face, her eyes filled with a sorrow that pierced through me. "You didn't come home" she said, her voice trembling. "I was terrified something had happened to you." There was something in her tone, an unspoken fear that ran deeper than my lateness. She knew—maybe she had always known—that I was restless, that I was searching for an escape, trying to leave the country. Her intuition was unerring, and though she didn't say it outright, I could feel her fear that tonight, I might not have come back at all.

I didn't have the heart to say much. Instead, I leaned down, kissed her gently on the cheek, and whispered, "Goodnight." Then I retreated to my room, my chest heavy with guilt and sorrow. It was only later, lying in bed, that her love truly hit me—the kind of boundless, all-consuming love only a parent can feel. She had spent the night convinced she had lost me forever, and that realization cut deep.

Still, as much as it pained me, I brushed it off. Fatigue overtook me, and I closed my eyes, letting sleep pull me away from the weight of her emotions. Before I left her, she had noticed my muddy clothes and asked, "What happened to you?"

I hesitated, unwilling to admit the truth of my clumsiness or the path I was on. Instead, I crafted a story. "Some of the boys from the village," I said. "We were playing a game, and it got rough. They pushed me near the creek. That's all."

She didn't press further, though her eyes lingered on me as if she didn't quite believe my tale. I knew she wasn't convinced, but I was too tired to say more. As I drifted off to sleep, her love weighed heavily on me. It was a painful, bittersweet thing to realize just how deeply she feared losing me—and how close that fear was to becoming a reality.

Chapter 3

The Day of the Escape

I had spent months toiling away in the rock quarry, working under the watchful eyes of the villagers. Over time, their perception of me softened; they believed I had reformed and began treating me as a respectable member of the community. Yet, despite this newfound acceptance, one door remained firmly shut: the door to education. For me, it was locked forever, an unspoken reminder of my supposed inadequacies.

Though I was outwardly accepted, whispers of doubt lingered. When I spoke of my burning desire to escape Albania, even daring to suggest bringing a friend along, my plans were met with scorn and rejection. "You belong behind bars," they would say. "You're not clever enough to succeed." Their words stung, but they also fueled my resolve. I dreamed of freedom constantly, my mind obsessing over every possible path to escape. Then, one day, an opportunity presented itself—a school excursion near the border, perfectly timed with the end of the school term. Something told me this might be the day.

That morning, the air felt different. The sun bathed the landscape in a golden glow, and the world seemed unusually calm, almost surreal. As I walked uphill to work, I stopped at a place called *Qiranica,* a cold-water creek where my grandfather had passed away many years ago after drinking from its waters. I sat there, having an early breakfast, and couldn't shake the feeling that the day was special, disconnected somehow from the mundane reality of life. It was a gut instinct—a deep, unexplainable certainty that today would change everything.

When I arrived at the quarry, the usual hum of chatter among my coworkers was filled with a story that chilled me. Someone recounted how women washing clothes near a creek had died when capsules of dynamite accidentally exploded in their pockets. The explosives, used for breaking rocks in the quarry, were dangerous but easily accessible to me. For reasons I couldn't fully explain, I had developed a strange fascination with these capsules. I liked carrying them, not for any purpose but because possessing something so powerful gave me a sense of having an edge—something others didn't have. That day, however, I suddenly remembered I had left a couple of these capsules in the pocket of my work pants, which were now at home.

My heart sank. My mother had announced earlier that she planned to do laundry that day. In our village, laundry was an arduous process: boiling water in a large pot, scrubbing clothes with soap, and then beating them with a wooden spatula-like tool to shake off dirt. If she found those capsules, or worse, if they detonated, the consequences would be unthinkable. I had to act.

My supervisor that day was someone I recognized from my nighttime work in the wheat fields, a way I earned extra money. I approached him, feigning illness. Pressing my hand to my stomach, I told him I felt pale and unwell. He waved me off, granting me permission to leave. Without hesitation, I hurled my shovel and pickaxe into the bushes, as though I would never need them again. Clutching my stomach for effect, I walked until I was out of sight, then broke into a run.

I ran as though my life depended on it, my heart pounding, my breath labored, but my determination unwavering. In what felt like no time at all, I reached the area where my mother was washing clothes, about thirty minutes from home. She was bent over the makeshift washing station, her hands busy with the soapy fabric. Gasping for breath, I told her not to touch my work pants. She paused, puzzled but trusting, and set them aside. Relief washed over me—disaster averted. It was then, as I caught my breath, that I remembered the school excursion planned for that day. The realization struck like lightning—today was the perfect day to escape. My mother urged me to return to work, scolding me for shirking my duties, but I refused. Instead, I promised her I'd help in the garden later. She relented, her focus returning to the laundry. I told her I was heading toward the buses and would be back soon.

As I walked away, I felt the weight of my decision pressing down on me. This day, so strangely beautiful and surreal, felt like a turning point. I wasn't sure if I would follow through, but something deep inside told me that my life would never be the same again.

Chapter 4

Preparing for the Escape

I carefully chose a pair of pants—simple slacks that wouldn't attract suspicion. I avoided taking anything that might hint at my intentions. Documents, personal belongings, or anything that could alert my mother to my plans were out of the question. I knew that if she sensed something was amiss, she would intervene. The only items I allowed myself were two photographs: one of my family and one of myself, both casually lying around the house. My identification card, a small red book issued by the Albanian government, stayed behind. Retrieving it would have required asking my mother for an impossibility. I left it and everything else behind.

I departed with nothing more than the clothes on my back and a small stash I had prepared long ago. Deep in the woods, hidden beneath the foliage, was a bag containing a knife and a few personal items—things I'd kept ready for years, just in case this day ever came.

Wearing my alternate pants and carrying no identification, I made my way to the tavern, my heart heavy with the weight of what I was about to do. At the bar, I borrowed bottles of **raki**, Albanian moonshine, from the bartender, Bairo, promising to repay him with my next paycheck. Deep down, I knew I'd likely never return to settle the debt, but in that moment, the alcohol felt like the only source of courage I had for the uncertain journey ahead. With the bottles clutched tightly in my hands, I left the tavern and headed for the bus station, each step carrying me closer to the unknown.

Bairo, the bartender, was a man of average build with curly hair and a kind, approachable face. But beyond his appearance, it was his good-hearted nature that stood out most. From past interactions, Bairo knew me as someone reliable. I had borrowed from him before and always repaid my debts when payday arrived. His trust in me was a small but meaningful bond in a world where resources were scarce, and trust wasn't easily given.

I often think about the dynamics of that trust and how much it meant to workers like me. Life in the rock quarry was harsh, the labor grueling and relentless, but it came with one significant advantage: better pay than what villagers typically earned. The quarry, being a government-owned utility, offered fixed salaries, creating a stark contrast between the incomes of city workers and those of villagers.

In the villages, income was tied to production—how much grain was harvested or how many animals thrived that season. A bad year could mean no pay at all, leaving families to scrape by however they could. In contrast, my 1,500 leks per month from the quarry seemed like a fortune compared to the villagers' meager 300 leks in a good month. The disparity highlighted the rigid hierarchy of the communist system, where even slight economic advantages created significant differences in quality of life. Still, the extra pay didn't make life luxurious; it simply gave me a sense of stability that many others lacked. It meant I could afford small indulgences, like borrowing bottles of **raki** when I needed them, or repaying debts on time to keep relationships intact. For someone like Bairo, who served as a lifeline for workers needing a drink to forget their troubles or summon courage, trust was as valuable as the money exchanged.

When I asked Bairo for the bottles that day, he didn't hesitate. He handed them over without question, knowing my history of keeping my word. It was a small, unspoken agreement that reflected the solidarity of people trying to survive under the weight of the same oppressive regime. As I walked away from the tavern and toward the bus station, the weight of the bottles in my hands felt heavier than usual, not because of their physical weight, but because of the path they symbolized. I was leaving behind the familiarity of my life, the trust of people like Bairo, and the stability, however modest, that I had built in the quarry. Yet, I carried with me the courage the **raki** offered and the hope that this uncertain journey would lead to something greater.

That moment, small and seemingly inconsequential, reflected life under the communist regime: a constant balancing act of trust, survival, and sacrifice. It was one of the last glimpses of the world I was leaving behind, and the memory of it, like the trust I shared with Bairo, stayed with me as I stepped into the unknown.

...

At the station, I lingered, watching the world I knew pass me by. The streets, the people, even the rhythm of the day felt different. Everything seemed surreal, as if I were already separated from my surroundings. A heavy sense of finality pressed down on me. This was it—the moment where I left my life behind and stepped into the unknown.

With the alcohol dulling my fear and sharpening my resolve, I ascended the hill leading to the picnic spot where my classmates had gathered. Halfway up, I paused and looked back. Below, I could see my mother at the clothes bench, scrubbing laundry with mechanical precision. A wave of emotion surged through me. I wanted to go to her, to say goodbye, but I knew I couldn't. She had made it clear: if she ever discovered I was trying to escape, she would report me. Her love, though fierce, was bound by the unyielding loyalty expected under the regime. Swallowing the lump in my throat, I turned and kept climbing, cutting ties with my upbringing in a single step.

When I reached the picnic, I mingled briefly with my classmates, trying to appear calm. Under the guise of illness, I excused myself, promising to rejoin them later at the tavern. They were distracted by a soccer game in the valley below, giving me the perfect opportunity to slip away unnoticed. I headed for the border.

Chapter 5

The Escape

As I descended into the valley, the oppressive silence was shattered by the crunch of boots on dry leaves. Two soldiers emerged from the woods, their presence striking like a thunderclap in the stillness. My heart pounded violently, fear coursing through my veins and rooting me to the spot. Panic gripped me like a vice, and my mind raced with questions I couldn't answer. What could I say if they stopped me? Why was I here? Every suspicion the village harbored about me would surely become my undoing.

Desperation overpowered fear. With shaking hands, I reached into my bag and pulled out one of the bottles of raki—Albanian moonshine—a silent offering for peace. The bottle caught the faint sunlight filtering through the trees as I stretched it toward them, my hand trembling.

One soldier approached cautiously, his expression unreadable. He took the bottle, uncorked it, and sniffed before taking a quick swig. Without a word, he passed it to his companion, who followed suit.

"Enjoy this day," the first soldier said at last, his tone oddly casual. "It's a good one for an excursion." His words were almost friendly, as if we were strangers meeting on a harmless stroll. Without another glance, they turned and disappeared into the woods, their laughter fading into the rustling leaves.

Relief hit me like a tidal wave, and my legs nearly buckled beneath me. My body trembled as I fought to steady myself, the reality of what just happened sinking in. They had gone east, away from my path, granting me a fleeting chance to escape. Tightening my grip on the remaining bottles, I slung them securely over my shoulder and pressed forward, every step measured and deliberate.

At the edge of the valley, I paused and turned back, my eyes lingering on the familiar landscape—the swaying trees, the vibrant grass, the comforting smells of home. It was heartbreakingly beautiful, a reminder of everything I was leaving behind. Nostalgia and grief clawed at my chest, but I forced myself to turn away. The forest ahead promised both concealment and peril. There was no going back.

The creek ahead marked a pivotal decision point. To the right lay home—familiar, with all its struggles and dangers. To the left, the border beckoned, offering freedom at an unimaginable cost. My pulse quickened as I turned left without hesitation, heading toward the base of Raduch Mountain. I knew hesitation could mean death.

The terrain grew steeper and more treacherous with every step. The border loomed somewhere ahead, snaking through dense forests and rocky slopes. Every sound seemed magnified—the crunch of leaves, distant animal calls, the whisper of wind through the trees. My nerves were frayed, haunted by stories of escapees shot dead near these very paths, their bodies left as warnings.

As the sun set, the shadows deepened, casting eerie shapes across the landscape. The air was heavy with the scent of pine and earth, mingling with the sweat soaking my shirt. Each step was a calculated risk, my feet testing the unsteady ground. Exhaustion clawed at me, but determination kept me moving.

A sharp crack in the distance—was it gunfire? My heart froze, and I dropped flat to the ground, pressing myself into the dirt. The alcohol dulled my senses, making it harder to focus, but I forced myself to crawl forward. Each inch felt agonizingly slow, every noise a potential threat.

Voices. My stomach churned as I strained to listen. Were they close? Were they looking for me? The voices faded, but paranoia lingered. I couldn't tell if I had crossed the border or if I was still trapped on Albanian soil. The uncertainty gnawed at me.

Ahead, abandoned bunkers came into view—relics of the Albanian military. I tossed small rocks inside to test for occupants, but only silence greeted me. Creeping past them, I continued up the mountain, the terrain growing rougher and the air thinner. My hands bled from scraping against jagged rocks, and my knees were raw. Still, I pushed forward.

Twilight descended, shrouding the world in a dim, ghostly light. The forest seemed to close in, and every step forward felt like an act of rebellion—against fear, against exhaustion, against the regime. I strained to see a sign of the border, but the darkness revealed nothing.

As stars dotted the night sky, I clung to hope, fragile yet persistent. Each step was a defiance of the oppressive forces that sought to control me. The path ahead was uncertain, but I knew one thing: I couldn't stop. My survival depended on it.

Chapter 6

The Crossing

The dim evening light painted the rugged landscape with long, shifting shadows. My legs felt leaden, every step a struggle against exhaustion, but the thought of stopping was out of the question. In the distance, I spotted something unusual a weathered, wooden sign half-hidden by overgrown shrubs. Intrigued, I moved closer, my heart pounding with a mix of hope and dread.

Carved into the surface of the sign were faint letters: "SFRJ," written in bold Cyrillic script. My breath caught in my throat as the realization washed over me: I had crossed the border. These letters stood for the Socialist Federal Republic of Yugoslavia. Somehow, without knowing it, I had entered a new land, leaving Albania behind. Relief and fear coursed through me in equal measure. The suffocating vigilance of Albanian patrols was gone—the endless rules, the looming threat of being shot for trying to escape, all behind me. Here, there were no watchtowers, no soldiers pacing the border, no barking dogs sniffing for intruders. The silence was unnerving, a stark contrast to the chaos I had left. It was calm, almost peaceful, but also desolate.

I reached out and touched the letters on the sign, as though grounding myself in this new reality. The Cyrillic script was both foreign and familiar, its sharp lines a declaration of freedom and the unknown. This was no longer the iron grip of Enver Hoxha's Albania. It was Yugoslavia—a land I had heard about in whispers, a steppingstone toward freedom. But the carved letters also carried a quiet warning: this was an uncharted world, with its own dangers and uncertainties. In my mind, these letters symbolized freedom, the first tangible proof that I had succeeded in crossing the border. As I stood by the sign, catching my breath, my mind raced with questions. How far had I come? Was I truly safe now, or was danger just around the corner? I thought of the stories I had heard about Yugoslavia—how it was a land of relative freedom compared to Albania but still a place of bureaucracy and political tension. The Socialist Federal Republic was no utopia, but for me, it represented the possibility of escape, a steppingstone to something greater.

The terrain ahead was unlike anything I had encountered. The dense Albanian forests gave way to a barren expanse of rocky hills and scattered trees, their stunted branches twisting like weary survivors. The ground was uneven, dotted with patches of stubborn grass that clung to life between the stones. The air was cooler, sharper, and carried the faint, earthy scent of distant rain.

For the first time in what felt like forever, I felt the oppressive weight of Albania's communist regime begin to lift from my shoulders. The fear of being caught, the ever-present watchful eyes—it was all behind me. Yet, the unease didn't vanish. This new land, while free of patrols, was unwelcoming in its silence. The barren hills seemed to stretch endlessly, and the absence of human life was unsettling.

I sat down briefly, resting against a cold patch of earth. My mind raced with the gravity of what had just happened. In my bag, I carried only the essentials, items I had clung to for survival. Among them was a knife—a tool, a weapon, a symbol of fear. Its weight in my bag seemed heavier now, a reminder of the life I was trying to escape. I reached in, pulled it out, and stared at it for a moment before hurling it far into the darkness. The clatter of the blade against the rocky ground echoed faintly, swallowed quickly by the night. Letting go of the knife felt liberating, as though I had shed a layer of my past. Vulnerable without it, yes—but also lighter. I adjusted the straps of my bag and stood up, brushing the dirt from my clothes. My legs wobbled beneath me, exhaustion and adrenaline battling for control. The air was cool against my sweat-soaked skin, and I shivered as I turned my gaze forward.

...

The letters on the sign, "SFRJ," were now behind me, marking a boundary not just of geography but of life itself. I wiped the sweat from my brow, my breath steadying. This was it—the moment I had dreamed of and dreaded in equal measure. There was no turning back. I moved cautiously; each step deliberate. Without the cover of dense forests, I was exposed, a lone figure in a vast, alien landscape. The stillness made even my breathing sound loud, a sharp reminder of how vulnerable I was. There were no villages in sight, no flickering lights on the horizon, just a path winding into the unknown.

I remembered the stories of Jablanica, a small town just beyond the Albanian border, often spoken of as a haven for those who escaped. It was said to be a place where refugees found temporary safety, a waypoint on their journey to freedom. But as I scanned the horizon, there was no sign of it. Jablanica was out of reach, hidden behind the endless folds of the hills. I imagined what it might look like—a quiet village nestled against the mountains, its streets filled with people who had escaped the grip of Albania, carving out lives of cautious freedom. But for now, it was just an idea, a distant promise. My focus remained on the path ahead, the faint outline of a trail illuminated by the pale moonlight.

The rugged path stretched before me, winding through the barren landscape. Every step away from that sign felt like a step toward an uncertain future. My thoughts flickered to the life I had left behind. Were the soldiers already searching for me? Had my absence been noticed? And what of my family? Would they ever know what had become of me?

In Albania, life had been a prison—a place of constant surveillance and unrelenting fear. Here, in Yugoslavia, the air was freer, the land more open. Yet, it was far from safe. Yugoslavia had its own tensions, its own struggles, and I was a stranger here, a fugitive with no plan and no guarantees.

The silence around me was profound, the wilderness indifferent to my presence. The moonlight cast long shadows across the ground, turning every rock and tree into something more menacing. I felt exposed, vulnerable to the unknown dangers of this new land. I pressed on, my resolve hardening with each step. Jablanica was still just a name, a distant hope, but it represented something bigger—a chance to keep going, to survive. The path was daunting, the future uncertain, but I moved forward with determination. Whatever lay ahead, I would face it. Freedom demanded nothing less.

The thought of what lay behind me pushed me forward. I couldn't afford to linger, to second-guess, or to let exhaustion take over. Every step away from that sign felt like a step toward a life I had barely dared to dream of. Gathering my resolve, I squared my shoulders and stepped forward, leaving the sign—and all it symbolized—behind me. Whatever awaited, I was determined to face it head-on. Relief mingled with trepidation as I scanned my surroundings. The slope stretched out before me, rugged and barren, offering no immediate shelter or direction. My head throbbed, the alcohol still buzzing faintly in my system, making my thoughts sluggish and fragmented. I found a spot to sit, resting against the cold ground as he gravity of my crossing began to sink in. Albania had been a prison of vigilance and control, but here—here was something different. Yugoslavia, though still unknown, carried an air of possibility.

Chapter 7

The Surrender

I lingered there on the slope, caught between two worlds, uncertain of what lay ahead but profoundly aware of what I had left behind. Having spent a few moments basking in the relief of having successfully crossed to the other side, I began surveying my surroundings to determine my next move. On the horizon, I spotted a building with a camouflage-like exterior. Deciding to explore, I stood up and started walking in that direction, mentally rehearsing how I would surrender myself. In this unfamiliar country, surrounded by an unknown environment, I was grappling with the uncertainty of what to expect.

Approaching the front door, I uttered "Albanac, Albanian." The soldiers, who turned out to be Macedonian, looked at me with surprise as they ushered me into a room. Feeling hunger pangs, I conveyed my need for food, and they promptly brought me a hearty meal – chicken soup with a sizable chicken leg and French bread. The satisfaction of that meal etched itself into my memory; it was a highlight, a foreign country welcoming me with a nourishing feast after a perilous journey.

After a brief rest, an investigator from the city of Struga named Jordan entered the room. Jordan had an average build, standing at around 5'7", and while I can't clearly recall the exact style or direction of his hair, his appearance didn't leave an intimidating impression. He looked like an ordinary guy—nothing particularly menacing about his demeanor at first glance.

But appearances can be deceiving. Despite his unremarkable looks, Jordan carried himself with a certain brute force, a roughness that showed in his approach to dealing with my situation. He was abrupt, his words often sharp and cutting, as if he wielded them like a weapon. There was an unpredictability in his demeanor that kept me on edge, making it impossible to anticipate his next move or reaction.

Though he didn't look threatening, his actions and tone painted a different picture. There was a raw, forceful energy about him—a mix of impatience and dominance that made him difficult to confront or reason with. It wasn't his physical stature that left a mark, but the harsh and uncompromising way he carried himself.

He expressed his intent to ensure that I had indeed escaped Albania and proposed taking me back to the border for mapping. Agreeing to this, I hopped into a Jeep. Throughout the journey, he bombarded me with random questions, to which I, being just a kid, responded to the best of my knowledge.

However, the tone shifted when he accused me of being an Albanian spy. Despite my insistence that I was merely a kid who had escaped Albania for personal reasons, tensions escalated. As we neared the escape point, the car halted, and I was instructed to step out. The investigator demanded to know where I had escaped, and when I pointed to the location, he insisted I return. Defiantly, I refused, and that's when he pulled out a gun, pressing it against my head. Undeterred, I maintained my refusal even as he pulled the trigger, only to discover the gun was empty. The sound of the trigger popping echoed in the air, and I felt my knees give way beneath me. I gasped for breath, offering my life but steadfastly refusing to go back.

This harrowing episode left me questioning whether escaping Albania was the right decision. The gravity of the choice weighed heavily on me as I realized that life ahead was not going to be easy. Despite the doubts and the newfound depression, the decision had been made, and I had to carry the consequences with me for the rest of my life. The journey, it seemed, had taken an unexpected and challenging turn

After concluding our tour with the investigator, we embarked on a journey to the city of Struga, where I planned to spend my first night. Unbeknownst to me, my initial enthusiasm had waned, and I soon found myself in trouble for violating border laws. I was subsequently confined to a solitary cell furnished with metallic bunk beds and a thin blanket. This unexpected turn of events left me bewildered and uncertain about what the future held. Fatigued and emotionally drained, I lay down and drifted into a fitful slumber. In my dream, I was back in Albania, inside my own house, but an unrelenting chill gripped me. I desperately tried to warm myself at the stove, yet it seemed an insurmountable task.

...

I awoke abruptly, gasping for breath and overwhelmed by a profound sense of despair. It was only at this moment that the full weight of my decision hit me – I had left behind everything I knew, including my family, and there was no turning back. Struggling to breathe, I pounded on the cell door in a frantic panic. A guard soon appeared and reassured me that I had been intoxicated but would eventually be fine. This was the first time in my life I had ever been confined in such a manner, and I felt as though the walls were closing in on me.

Gazing out of the jail window, I heard people passing by. My attention was drawn to a young couple passionately kissing right in front of me, behind the bars. Observing their love for one another gave me a glimmer of hope, reminding me that life was worth living, despite the uncertain future that lay ahead. What made it even more daunting was the realization that I knew nothing about these people. My perceptions of Yugoslavians had been shaped solely by communist propaganda, and I had never truly understood who they were as individuals.

Chapter 8

The Confinement

I underwent several days of interviews at the facility, during which I was informed that I would soon be transferred to a sizable prison in Skopje, Macedonia, with an unspecified sentence duration. A few days later, they drove me for several hours until we reached Skopje. I recall the car coming to a halt in front of a facility concealed by overgrown branches, resembling an ancient castle. The massive front door loomed before me as I was led inside, my hands bound in handcuffs. While the exact details of my entry escape me, I do remember traversing lengthy, immaculate hallways with glistening floors and the occasional metallic doors that clanged shut as we passed through.

The prison bore similarities to jail but on a much grander scale. It remained predominantly solitary, and I rarely had the chance to explore its interior except for the occasions when I was escorted for interrogation. The atmosphere within was perpetually cold, and the quality of the food served was abysmal. Any preconceived notions I had about this place were swiftly shattered. It was heart-wrenching to witness fellow inmates suffering from severe coughing fits throughout the facility. I existed in solitude, and every morning brought with it the dread of another interrogation session.

I was acutely aware that I was lost, utterly clueless about their laws, the duration of my confinement, and the impending future. I recalled overhearing conversations back in Albania where people spoke of escapees suffering torture and even losing their lives in Yugoslavian prisons. They described harrowing accounts of individuals being burned with cigarette butts, subjected to beatings, whippings, and confinement in dark, damp cells. It left me feeling profoundly adrift.

As evening descended and darkness enveloped me, tears welled up in my eyes. I found myself questioning why

I had ever attempted to escape, berating myself for believing the promises of respectful treatment upon reaching Yugoslavia. The reality did not match the bias I had been led to believe. I cried and closed my eyes, desperately yearning for more comforting thoughts and a place in my mind where I could seek solace.

I reminisced about a time long ago, during my ninth-grade education in the city of Durres, Albania. To gain admission to the school, students needed exemplary grades. A scholarship originally intended for my friend, who had ranked first in our class, had been redirected to me since he declined it due to its focus on mechanical agriculture. My family had a favorable standing as veterans, owing to my uncle's sacrifice in the Nazi war, which spared us undue political scrutiny. My departure had cast a shadow on our reputation, but in those days, my family enjoyed a degree of prestige. They reveled in their status as a veterans' family, and the communists did not subject them to harsh treatment.

My uncle, my mother's brother, resided in or near the city of Durres. He frequently regaled me with tales of his longing to escape to a country free from dictatorship, where human dignity and decency were upheld throughout society. His stories were so compelling that they ignited a desire in me to learn more about the possibility of escaping. I fondly recall how he used to take me along to the beach, where we would swim, savor a special cucumber and feta cheese salad with fresh tomatoes, and enjoy a beer while basking in relaxation. Albania's beaches were truly picturesque, boasting top-quality sand that provided a delightful place to recline.

As I languished in my cell, my thoughts drifted back to those serene beach days, offering a semblance of comfort. In my mind, I was falling asleep on the beach when the cell door abruptly slammed shut. A guard had arrived to deliver supper, consisting of a meager serving of thin soup and a quarter of a French bread. Hunger gnawed at me, but I couldn't help but resent being forcibly torn away from the tranquil mental escape I had crafted for myself.

After supper, I returned to the cold, hard bunk bed, laid my head on the pillow, and sought to find sleep. I remained oblivious to when they would awaken us or when the next round of questioning would commence. As I lay there, I found myself drifting back into my past, revisiting my days at the mechanical agricultural school.

I vividly recalled the first day when we were assigned to the dorms, and I had the opportunity to make new friends. In those dormitories, there were about 20 beds in a single room, with some students occupying the upper bunks and others on the lower ones. It was an uncomfortable experience for me because I had never been in such a communal living situation, and there was an inherent sense of survival in the dynamics. Initially, I struggled to forge connections. Coming from a village and being thrust into this unfamiliar environment, I often withdrew for weeks at a time. Being a first-year student, I had yet to establish many acquaintances, and I felt utterly lost at the outset.

The teacher in charge of my class was a member of the Communist Party, and many years later, after Albania transitioned to democracy, he assumed the role of Mayor of Durres Albania. The school consisted of the main building, followed by a hall, a mess hall, and then the dormitories in the rear. Despite feeling adrift as a young student, I eventually began making friends outside the school and delved into some illicit activities to earn money. It was during this time that I crossed paths with a young lady named Liliana, who hailed from our region, and our shared heritage added a unique bond to our friendship. It was also the period when I first experimented with smoking and drinking. Instead of attending school, I would spend my time with Liliana and her friends, engaging in activities that children were not supposed to be involved in.

My academic journey was far from successful, and eventually, I failed my classes, leading me to return home. It was during this time that I encountered a group of individuals who were vehemently anti-government. Some of their relatives had been imprisoned, and I found myself drawn to their cause. Among them was a distant cousin of mine and his wife, who resided in a small village near my school, and I began visiting them regularly. Through these connections, I encountered other individuals who were considered dangerous by the authorities. One of them had recently been released from prison for his opposition to the communist government.

One day, in a casual conversation with one of my cousins, I jokingly remarked that this recently released individual might actually want to go back to prison. Little did I know, a few days later, a group of his friends abducted me, taking me to a secluded cornfield where they brutally assaulted me, leaving me naked and terrified. Astonishingly, no charges were ever filed against them, though the experience left me deeply shaken. I found myself wondering why I had gotten involved in such trouble, and this frightening incident remained etched in my memory.

Lying on the bunk bed in my current confinement, I tossed and turned, struggling to find a comfortable position for the night in the hope of obtaining some much-needed rest.

Chapter 9

First Day of Torture

The door creaked open, and I heard the guard delivering my breakfast. It consisted of a piece of bread, a small inch-sized portion of cheese, and a cup of tea. I woke up with the resignation that I was still confined to the cell, and the day was about to begin. I hastily consumed the breakfast and got dressed, then lay on the bed, awaiting whatever would come next. Rest had eluded me, and I sat there in anticipation of the uncertain future. Time seemed to drag on slowly, and there were moments when it felt like nothing would happen, leaving me in an endless state of waiting – a truly disconcerting thought.

Surveying the cell walls, I noticed various drawings left by different individuals who had been here before me. I decided to add my name to this makeshift gallery, thinking that if anyone I knew came later, they would recognize that I had been here.

As I waited, my thoughts drifted back to the past, to a time when I was expelled from school. I vividly remembered sending my younger brother to fetch some wine from the local club. During his visit, he encountered a group of people who taunted him about me. Enraged, I marched to the club, and in a fit of anger, I challenged anyone who dared to confront me, declaring that if they wanted to face their demise, they should step forward. Some believed I was insane, but I knew I was merely thrust into the forefront to protect the reputation of our village and my peers. Being suspended from school seemed like a dead-end, and I had to resort to whatever means were necessary.

After being awake for several hours, the door finally creaked open. I could hear the jingling of keys, indicating that this was a different kind of service, and then came the arrival of food. It was a tall gentleman with bulging muscles and a prominent nose. He called my name and said, "Ilir, come with me." I obediently followed him a few doors down the hallway, moving toward the entrance, and then I was led into a room. The room was devoid of windows, its walls covered in ominous black leather cloth that sent a shiver down my spine. I couldn't help but conclude that this room was likely used for interrogations.

The gentleman introduced himself as Nicola, my interrogator. He instructed me to sit in a chair, positioning himself across from me. Before I could comprehend his intentions, I felt his large hands forcibly wiping my face, causing an immediate headache and a nosebleed.

"Let's get this straight," he said sternly. "I'll be asking you questions, and you will answer them as I ask them." I nodded, indicating my readiness to cooperate, but I couldn't understand why he needed to keep me in this unsettling environment. "Tell me, who are you, and why did you come here?" Nicola continued. I replied with my name and explained that I had escaped Albania in search of a better life. He pressed further, asking, "Who sent you?"

"Nobody sent me. I didn't have any paperwork with me because my mother was washing my clothes that day, and I couldn't risk her discovering my escape plans by finding such documents, " I replied honestly Nicola sat in silence for a moment, his expression skeptical, before finally stating, "I don't believe you."

Suddenly, a sharp blow struck my face, not just any blow, but a flurry of blows like searing stars. The impact was immediate, causing an intense headache, followed by another strike on the opposite side. In agony, I heard the interrogator accusingly demand, "Liar! Who sent you?" Tears welled up in my eyes, not from intentional crying but from the sheer pain and disbelief that I was now subjected to torture in Macedonia. It became alarmingly evident that there was truth to the rumors about their brutal interrogation techniques. What sent chills down my spine was the uncertainty of how far they would go to harm me. Fear gripped me, and I found my voice, pleading, "Sir, you're hurting me. I've told you everything truthfully. Please, stop hurting me. I fear I may not survive if you strike me again."

Suddenly, I felt a vice-like pinch on my index finger, his grip unyielding, and for a terrifying moment, I thought he might snap the joint. The pain was excruciating, and I implored, "Sir, please, why did I escape Albania? This is not necessary."

The questioning lasted for approximately two hours, and I vividly recall enduring physical discomfort throughout the remainder of the day. I was subjected to pinching, pushing, slapping, and even having my toes stepped on, and my recollection of the specific events has become hazy. Nevertheless, the day was undeniably brutal, and I struggled to comprehend why anyone would subject a child to such treatment. My mental energy had been completely drained, and I was eventually escorted out of the interrogation room and placed in a cell. My memories of the afternoon slowly faded, but what remained clear was the profound hardship I had endured as I was forcibly dragged down the hallway and unceremoniously deposited in the cell.

I found myself in the cell, overwhelmed by dizziness. As I glanced around, it felt as though the world had closed in on me. Summoning every ounce of strength I could muster; I managed to climb onto the bunk bed. I imagined it was a beautiful day outside, with my friends, the cohort slated for graduation, engaged in a spirited game of soccer. Our team was victorious, and we cheered each other on with resounding chants. It felt as if the soccer ball moved precisely at my command, and our competitive class always gave their best on the field.

After sending the soccer ball towards the goal, I suddenly found myself drifting onto the lush green grass in a valley near the border. This was a special place where villagers gathered for excursions every year, and sheepherders set up camps during the winters. The valley was surrounded by magnificent oak trees that stretched for miles, providing shade and a perfect spot for relaxation. The grass was incredibly inviting for lounging.

I ran and played with my friends, and even my childhood friend Lily was there that day. It was carefree enjoyment, a day filled with sports, food, and camaraderie. However, everything took an unexpected turn when a soccer ball struck me on the head, causing pain and confusion. I reached for my head, feeling my bumps and realized I was awake.

I looked around and saw daylight, resembling the morning. In one corner of the cell, there were two trays of food—one from last night's dinner and the other from this morning's breakfast. I had been unconscious for almost 16 hours. Fear started to creep in as I scanned the cell. What if I never escaped this place? Struggling to get up to use the bathroom, I realized the difficulty due to the numerous bumps and bruises all over my body. As I removed my shirt, I discovered a streak on my chest, almost like a signature of a whip, and there was a hint of blue in the marks as well.

Despair hung heavy in the air as I brought myself back to reality. All my efforts to reach freedom seemed futile. What if no one knew where I was? These were daunting thoughts, and I felt foolish for my actions. This day would forever be etched in my memory. I had been beaten and tortured by the UDB, the Yugoslavian intelligence agency, a fact that was becoming painfully clear.

I positioned myself in the center of the room in front of the bed, I hesitated. Uncertainty gnawed at me; I couldn't determine if I was hungry or if I wanted to consume the food that had been sitting out overnight. In that moment, food held no allure for me. I slowly returned to the bed and reclined on my back; my gaze fixed on the ceiling. A lantern hung from the middle of the ceiling, casting intermittent shadows. I shifted my gaze from the ceiling to the walls and then to the door.

The atmosphere in that room was grim, and I desperately sought refuge in my mind, searching for memories of better times. I strained to transport myself to a mental place where wonderful memories resided, a realm almost like science fiction where everything fell into place, and I held control. However, I struggled to find that mental escape because the harsh reality of my surroundings held me captive.

I recalled a time, long ago, when I was around ten years old, and the world felt like an endless canvas of possibilities. Winter had transformed our little village into a magical wonderland, the snow blanketing everything in a soft, pristine white. The air was crisp, sharp enough to bite but exhilarating as it filled my lungs. The snow was untouched, glistening under the pale light of a distant sun, and when I ran across the frozen surface, it felt as if I could fly. There were no boundaries, no obstacles—just the smooth, icy terrain that carried me wherever my heart desired. Our village was often buried beneath five to ten feet of snow, turning the landscape into an endless playground. The rooftops blended seamlessly into the hills, and the roads disappeared beneath a sparkling sea of white. The smooth, icy crust of the snow was perfect for gliding, sliding, and losing ourselves in endless games. As the sun set, casting a golden glow over the horizon, my friends and I would stay outside, our laughter echoing into the night.

Among my friends was Lily, a girl who had always stood out to me in a way I couldn't yet fully understand. She was beautiful, with dark curls that peeked out from beneath her woolen hat and eyes that seemed to hold secrets of their own. Her laugh was as warm as the firelight we'd gather around after hours of play, and her smile could light up even the coldest, darkest evenings. We shared a special bond, an unspoken connection that felt like it had existed forever. I was drawn to her, not just because of her beauty, but because of the way she made everything seem more vibrant and alive. When we played together, it wasn't just a game—it was an adventure. We'd race across the frozen snow, her scarf trailing behind her like a ribbon in the wind, and for a moment, I felt like we were the only two people in the world.

I remember one night in particular. The moon hung low and full, casting a silver glow over the landscape, and the stars seemed to shimmer just for us. Lily and I had wandered a little further from the others, our breath fogging in the icy air as we talked and laughed. She picked up a handful of snow and tossed it at me, her laughter ringing out like a melody. I couldn't help but smile as I retaliated, and soon, we were chasing each other, our footsteps marking the untouched snow in a pattern only we could decipher. When we finally stopped, breathless and rosy-cheeked, she looked at me with those bright eyes of hers, and I felt something stir in my chest. It was a feeling I didn't fully understand then—a warmth that seemed to melt away the cold around us. I didn't have the words to describe it at the time, but looking back, I know it was the first time I felt the stirrings of love.

Even now, years later, that memory remains vivid, like a page torn from the storybook of my childhood. It's a reminder of a simpler time when the world was blanketed in snow, and my heart was just beginning to understand the depth of its own emotions. During those evenings, we would wrestle, run around, and engage in various games. These moments represented the epitome of childhood joy. Despite the scarcity of food and material possessions in the communist system, we cherished the opportunity to socialize. Every evening, people of all age groups would gather, forming their own associations, and fostering a strong sense of community.

I remember that, early on, I resorted to sneaking some wine from the bushes to become more sociable. I was often subjected to hurtful words from others, and alcohol seemed to be the answer to my social insecurities. Once I started drinking, I felt like I could fit in anywhere and do anything, including those exhilarating nights of running on the endless, frozen snow. At some point, it even felt like I could run forever. Despite my persistent hunger, my physical health was robust during my childhood.

During those days, I excelled as a student. I consistently earned high grades in school, and my father expressed his pride in my academic achievements. However, something remarkable occurred after I completed the fourth grade—it felt as though a light had been switched on, and suddenly, I comprehended everything I read, excelled in mathematics, and stood out as the best in English and many other subjects. While my friends devoted significant time to studying and consistently performed well, for me, it all seemed to come effortlessly. I would study, and the result was either an A or a perfect 10, but if I didn't put in the effort, I would receive an F. I was often told that I possessed great intelligence, but I was cautioned that without regular study and consistent effort, I might not succeed. I set out to prove them wrong, and I did just that. In the end, I earned excellent grades, surpassing the efforts of my peers.

The feeling of receiving compliments for my intelligence was exhilarating. I remember being more interested in reading extensive books, such as Rembrandt's 700-page tome, than the required class readings I had to defend in front of the classroom at times. However, my academic journey was a mixed bag, influenced by the events in my life and the pressures I faced. Nevertheless, I excelled in school from the fourth to the eighth grade.

...

The door suddenly made a metallic sound as it swung open, and the guard entered the cell. He glanced at the untouched food, then picked up the trays and left the room. He stood there for a moment, looking at me with what seemed like sympathy in his eyes. I turned onto my left side on the bunk bed, desperately trying to make an effort to ignore the guard's presence. As the door clanged shut behind me, tears began to well up.

Here was the food that I could have eaten, now gone. It didn't affect me too deeply because I knew it was my own choice that led to this outcome. The guard was not my parent, and it was my decision, so I accepted it, but I couldn't help feeling regretful that I was locked up without being a criminal.

Lying on my side, I drifted back into the past, reminiscing about our village. There was a central street, unpaved but in my eyes, it was like the most beautiful boulevard in the world. It connected the village center to the shops on the eastern side of the village. On that side, there were stables where the government kept livestock, along with depots for food and bread. This was where we obtained our supplies in the evening.

Every evening around 7:00 PM, we would line up to receive fresh bread allocated to the villagers. Everything was rationed—bread, cheese, meat. In the communist regime, there were no personal belongings like vehicles or large machines; these were all government-owned. Those who held influence were the ones in control of essential commodities like bread, milk, meat, and cheese. This is where corruption thrived. When you were hungry and had no access to these items, they became valuable commodities. The party leaders had these goods delivered to their homes, while the rest of us struggled to obtain enough because they couldn't provide sufficient quantities. Corruption was pervasive, whether it involved food or something of greater value. Such was life in Albania.

I turned onto my back and rolled to the right, attempting to get up. Slowly, I made my way towards the sink adjacent to the bathroom stall. The sink had a metallic, aluminum appearance, and the mirror was also made of metal. Although the reflection in the metal mirror lacked the clarity of a regular mirror, I could still see myself somewhat clearly. I stood in front of it, examining my pale skin and disheveled hair. In the days since my escape, I had endured a great deal, and my face appeared thinner. I stood there for a moment, gazing at the reflection of a weary and powerless individual. Incarceration was an entirely new experience for me.

Chapter 10

The Interrogation Continues

My thoughts were interrupted by a knock on the door, and a short man with curly brown hair named George asked me to follow him. It was the second day of interrogations, and I couldn't help but feel anxious about what would come next. I complied and followed George, taking the opportunity to study the surroundings in my head as we walked down the hallway. However, George urged me to hurry, so I refocused on following him.

I was led into a different room than the one from the previous day, and I found myself in a smaller room. In the center of the room, there was a chair, and a bar-like setup. Nicola was standing in the corner, and I was startled as he greeted me with a simple "hello there." Both men were now seated across from me.

"I want you to tell George how you escaped Albania again," Nicola instructed, and I began recounting my escape story.

"Do you believe him, George?" Nicola inquired, to which George responded, "No, I don't. We have sources in Albania, in the village of klenja, and we were told that you are a spy."

"I assure you, I'm not," I responded urgently, my heart pounding.

"That may be true or not, because it's not," George said, suddenly moving behind me and grabbing my hair. The pain was excruciating. "The sooner you tell us who you are and what you're doing here, the quicker we'll get this done."

"I've told you everything," I insisted. "There's nothing more to tell."

George moved right in front of me and lit a cigarette. "You know, if you don't tell us the truth, we have other ways," he warned, holding the cigarette dangerously close to my hand. "You'd better tell me the truth because I'm going to place this cigarette on your wrist, and if you've never experienced it before, you don't want to."

"Please, you guys are really hurting me," I pleaded. "I've told you everything there is to tell, and even if you kill me, there's nothing more I can tell you. I can't even lie to you because you don't even know what a lie is."

I felt George punch me on the top of my head with his fist, causing intense pain. The rest of the day was a blur as I was threatened and subjected to further pain, and it became clear that they had no mercy. The guards forcefully grabbed me by the hair and escorted me back to my cell. I lay down, not wanting to move, but the gnawing hunger in my stomach eventually compelled me to get up.

After a while, the door clanged open, and a tray of soup with potatoes, leeks, and a quarter of a French bread was brought in. I slowly rose and devoured it all, satisfying my hunger for the moment. As I sat on the bunk bed, I noticed that all I had in the cell was a small pillow and a thin blanket. The cold seeped through my bones as I lay there, and the meager blanket offered little warmth. I glanced around the room and gradually drifted into my memories. I recalled my early days, born prematurely shortly after my mother brought me home. The doctors had predicted I wouldn't arrive for another seven weeks, but I surprised everyone. I was the fifth child in a family of six brothers, and my mother had previously experienced the loss of a stillborn baby girl. From a very young age, our family had a competitive spirit among its members.

My father, an intelligent man, held a position in charge of the supply chain. It was a significant role that could have brought prosperity to our family, but his struggle with alcoholism rendered him ineffective at home, although his work benefited the world.

My mother worked tirelessly for the government, herding cattle. She would rise at six in the morning and return home at ten at night. Her life was marked by cruelty and hardship. I always tried to fend for myself and, at times, resorted to stealing to stave off hunger. Sometimes, I would sneak away with friends to pilfer food to avoid my family turning me in. Despite our dire circumstances and hunger, my family remained resolute in upholding the law and living an honest life. Consequently, I often had to operate outside their knowledge to ensure my own survival.

I have a vivid memory of a summer when I was seventeen years old. I had taken on a job with the cooperative to safeguard the wheat. The task required me to sleep next to the wheat piles in the middle of the Klenja field. They believed I was doing an excellent job protecting the wheat, but it came with its own set of risks, primarily the threat of being devoured by wolf packs in the area. My motivation for taking on this role wasn't solely the money the cooperative paid me; it was because I had formed alliances with villagers from neighboring villages. They relied on me to secure wheat for their livelihoods, paying me in return. These villagers would sneak in at night to load their horses with wheat, potatoes, or anything they could find in the piles I was supposed to safeguard. I made a substantial amount of money from this arrangement, and I would often venture to nearby villages to spend my earnings at the tavern, drinking the day away until I was as intoxicated as could be.

In my mind, those were good days, as they allowed me to drink cognac and various other spirits, providing a means to escape from reality. This escapism was rooted in my desire to keep my family unaware of what I possessed and what I was involved in. The drinking did take its toll on me, but I yearned to forget reality and simply enjoy life. At some level, I had always been in an escape mode, looking for a way out, much like my current situation, though this time it wasn't going as well.

Restlessly, I began pacing in the cell, overcome by tears. I had always been a free man, and now, here I was, unsure of where this ordeal would ultimately lead me. I endured torture during my time in Macedonia, subjected to grueling beatings for fifteen consecutive days. Each day blended into the next, and I watched as I steadily lost weight, gazing at my gaunt reflection in the cold metallic mirror across the cell. Life in that jail was an unrelenting ordeal.

Chapter 11

Time in Solitary Confinement

As the days passed, the treatment did improve, and by the fifteenth day, I was no longer subjected to torture or questioning. Nicola informed me that in Yugoslavia, the penalty for illegal entry into the country was thirty days in prison, which meant I would soon be released. This revelation brought a sense of relief and renewed hope, but the scars of torture remained.

I had celebrated my nineteenth birthday while in that Macedonian cell. The rest of my days in confinement were long, filled with reflection. Looking back on my life, I began to understand more about myself. I realized that I had always been someone who moved quickly through life, never taking the time to truly understand myself. Life in that jail cell had become monotonous. There was little interaction with anyone except for the guards during mealtimes. The cell offered no other options or activities, making it feel like true solitary confinement. I would occasionally get up, pace around the cell, and then return to the bed. There was a man in the neighboring cell who couldn't stop coughing. It seemed like he was unable to tolerate the harsh conditions and was getting increasingly ill.

As I looked at the left wall, I noticed a list with many names on it. I decided to add my own: "Ilir Nina has been here. Klenje, Albania." Memories of my school days flooded my mind. I reminisced about being around fourteen years old, attending class with my classmates. We were all eighth-grade graduates and formed a tight-knit group. I was among the top students in the class, boasting high marks. I ranked second in the class, just behind Alex. He was a dedicated student, and we were okay friends. We often helped each other with schoolwork, solving various academic puzzles together and expanding our knowledge.

Indeed, Alex eventually pursued a path to law school, opting to abandon an agricultural mechanic scholarship that had originally been awarded to him. As a second choice, the scholarship was then graciously offered to me. Our classroom fostered a vibrant social life, and we often gathered to prepare for various volunteer activities.

One evening remains vivid in my memory—the night of our class dance. Our class comprised roughly fifteen boys and ten girls, and among them was my dear friend Lily. She appeared absolutely stunning in her green dress adorned with white stripes. Summoning all my courage, I mustered the words to ask her for a dance, and to my delight, she graciously accepted my invitation. Her smile was truly irresistible, causing her cheeks to rise in tandem with her captivating green eyes. Each moment of that dance was a cherished memory, and I couldn't help but allow my mind to wander, envisioning a future where I could marry her and spend the rest of my life by her side.

In Albania, however, love alone wasn't enough. To marry someone, you need to be financially well-off and come from a respectable family. Being a good provider was a prerequisite, and your family had to have no political affiliations or issues with the government. Family stability also played a significant role. I knew that my chances were slim, but I couldn't help but feel and imagine a different future. That evening marked the final dance of our eighth-grade year, and none of us knew where life would lead us next. Some would continue their education in the village, while others, like me, would pursue opportunities elsewhere, such as the agricultural mechanic school.

I was roused from my thoughts by the sound of the door cracking open. It was the guard delivering my meal. We had very little interaction in this place, and these brief encounters with the guards during mealtime were almost the only human contact I had. I got up from my bed, picked up the tray of food, and examined what was on it. Tonight's supper consisted of a quarter of a French bread and a hearty potato stew with beef, garnished with a rich red sauce. The stew was surprisingly tasty, but it was far from enough to satisfy my ever-present hunger.

As I sat there, my mind was filled with a growing sense of impatience to be free from this facility. Although I knew that my release would come eventually, I had developed this nagging belief that I might never see the light of day outside these walls again. My outlook on life had drastically changed during my time here, and my once-boundless enthusiasm had been crushed. I felt like a stranger in my own skin, knowing nothing about the outside world—the lifestyle, beliefs, thoughts, or social norms. I was thrust into the unknown, and so far, it hadn't been a pleasant journey.

I moved to the bathroom area and stood before the metallic mirror, absentmindedly touching my face and running my fingers through my hair. There wasn't much to see on the other side. I could feel tears welling up in my eyes, a stark reminder of how I had seemingly vanished from the world I once knew.

Memories of my village school flooded back to me. It was just a short five-minute walk from my house, situated on the main street, the only street, in fact. As you left my home and turned right onto the main street, it was a quick five-minute journey to the schoolyard. The school comprised two buildings facing each other. The right side was just a portion of the front, while the left side extended towards a creek where we would stand at attention and start our school day.

The principal, undoubtedly a staunch communist, would deliver his daily speech, reflecting whatever the Communist Party wanted to emphasize that day. We would then engage in morning exercises, with some students doing physical activities while others went for a run further south. Around 9:00, we would be led into our classrooms one by one. Each building was made of rock and housed approximately six classrooms, each of which was simple, with student benches and a blackboard. There were no frills or extras; it was a place of learning.

I enjoyed my time in school, and under the communist regime, as long as you didn't challenge the government, you were left relatively unbothered. However, you had to follow orders and be cautious about what you said. I recalled a particular incident during my eleventh grade when I had written "WC" on the 8th Congress book. That day, on my way to school, I noticed several vehicles from the security services and the principal waiting for me. They pulled me aside and escorted me to the principal's office.

`Inside the office, it was the principal, the vice-principal, and an operative from the security services. They confronted me about the writing in the book and asked if I had done it. I instinctively denied it, knowing that admitting guilt would land me in trouble. I mentioned that my family had a history of veterans, and I wouldn't engage in such actions. The interrogation lasted for about four hours, and it was a close call. I was relieved that I hadn't confessed, as it could have had severe consequences. However, one of my friends, Andy, was wrongly blamed for it and suffered because of his marked family background, with relatives who had escaped to Yugoslavia.

My presence in Albania after that incident made me a target for scrutiny, and I knew they were digging for anything they could use against me. I had been a reckless child, unaware of the potential consequences. Even at 16 years old, I could have been imprisoned for life. It was like playing with fire in a country where free speech was a luxury, and one wrong word could lead you down a perilous path. Sometimes, in retrospect, I wondered if I would have been better off dealing with the consequences there than enduring the hardships I faced in Yugoslavia in my pursuit of freedom.

I made my way to the bunk bed, exhausted from the day's ordeal, and attempted to find a comfortable resting position. As I lay there, my mind wandered back to a time in the past, during an election season in our village. It was a memorable occasion when the villagers would gather to ignite a massive fire atop the Osoi mountain, a tradition observed on communist holidays or during election days. This mountain held great significance as it was adorned with communist slogans made of white rocks, proudly displayed for all to see. The trek to the summit took about forty-five minutes, and I had the opportunity to participate in gathering enough wood and starting the fire. I vividly recalled the grandeur of the scene—the slogans on the mountain, the roaring fire at the peak, and the people descending with torches to show their unwavering support for the Communist Party. The crowd would chant loudly, "Long live the Communist Party!" and various other slogans. This event took place around 1987, after the passing of Enver Hoxha, the dictator, but the communist system remained firmly in place.

I had spent approximately three hours helping build the fire alongside the leaders who organized the event. The mountain's peak was barren, devoid of trees, but there were trees about 500 feet away, making it a suitable location for a fire without the risk of it spreading to the nearby oak trees. The sight of the torches lighting up the night sky as people ascended and descended the mountain was truly magnificent. Afterward, we would march through the village and along the main street, still chanting slogans. It was a clear message from the Communist Party: "You must support the elections." Failure to do so was seen as aiding Yugoslavia and imperialist America. None of the villagers dared to vote against the communist party; they maintained a stranglehold on the election process. The Communist Party proudly claimed to have 100% of the vote, and anyone who voted otherwise risked imprisonment for not supporting communist Albania.

The dictatorship had taken a severe toll on the people, especially over two generations, who struggled to make a living. The regime allowed individuals to possess only one cow and one donkey, and nothing more. This was the norm for villages, and for the cities, ownership was even more restricted, limited to just a bicycle. The communists controlled the population through commissars, partisan leaders, and administrators, with the Communist Party holding ultimate authority. Their slogan, "The party is above all," underscored their dominance.

Despite the harsh reality of life under communism, those torch-lit gatherings were a beautiful sight to behold. It was a time when we could connect with friends and, in our own small ways, attempt to defy the constraints of the system. We were energetic kids trapped within the confines of the communist regime. People maintained an outward appearance of honesty, but it was often out of fear, as no one could freely express their true thoughts or feelings. The constraints were suffocating, and life in the village was all I knew.

I had visited cities a few times, but being a rural native, I couldn't fully grasp the challenges faced by city-dwellers under the communist regime. I could only assume that they endured similar propaganda and restrictions. For the slightest transgressions, children were sent to prison, and lives were forever tainted by false accusations. Albania was in dire straits, and perhaps that was one of the reasons why I longed to escape the country, to explore and understand the wider world beyond its borders.

I lay on my back in the cramped jail cell, my thoughts drifting to a different time and place. The cell was not particularly spacious, measuring about three meters in height, two meters in width, and roughly 4 meters in depth. It's rough, unpaved interior was constructed from concrete blocks, providing minimal insulation from the extreme temperatures outside. It was a stark environment, and my mind sought solace in memories of the past.

It was a Saturday, and I was just sixteen years old. It was the potato season, but I had stopped attending school because I had failed to make the grade at the mechanical agricultural school and was back in the village. Instead, I found myself on the Main Street, observing the buses that would transport my friends and other villagers to volunteer in the potato fields. My friends were diligently following the routine, continuing to attend school while also participating in communal efforts.

I decided to join them on their journey eastward to the Klenja field. I hadn't even brought lunch with me, but that didn't deter me. One of the communist members overseeing the endeavor recognized my willingness to volunteer and praised my spirit. Despite my academic setbacks, he expressed hope for my future if I remained committed to the ideals of the communist government.

Throughout the day, we toiled in the fields, harvesting potatoes. By day's end, there were massive piles of potatoes ready for transportation to other areas. My role continued into the night as I stood guard over these piles, ensuring they weren't pilfered. I even took it upon myself to sell some of the potatoes to neighboring communities.

The day was enjoyable as I bonded with friends, connected with my peers, and tried to get closer to Lily. The communists managed to infuse these events with a sense of camaraderie and purpose, acknowledging the efforts of the people, even though the government was taking the potatoes without compensation.

Amidst the sense of unity, there was a particular friend and cousin within our group who repeatedly picked fights with me. We would often find ourselves away from the others, and he would launch punches at me. Although he had a significant size advantage, I had speed on my side. Our confrontations resembled a cat-and-mouse game: he would strike, and I would swiftly retaliate with a stick or a rock before evading him once more. Over time, our clashes left both of us bloodied and battered.

Despite his physical superiority, I never backed down. He was a bully who struck fear into many, including myself, but I consistently confronted him, even though I was aware that I was no match for him. I was a small, short kid with limited body mass, facing off against a giant bully. I endured these battles on my own, as my older brothers avoided conflicts with his counterparts. This was partly because the bully had a brother the same age as my other two siblings, and they preferred to stay out of it.

One morning, tensions escalated as this kid mouthed off, and I seized a rock, hurling it at his back. It struck him, and he bled from the impact. He threatened to kill me the next time we crossed paths, but that fight marked the end of our clashes. He had come to believe that I was utterly unpredictable and perhaps even a bit unhinged.

The fear he felt in my presence, combined with the unpredictable nature of our confrontations, ultimately put an end to our ongoing rivalry. It was a challenging period, and I was often seen as the underdog, but my determination to stand up to the bully remained unwavering.

I tossed and turned in my uncomfortable bunk, desperately trying to find a position that would offer some semblance of rest. I had lost track of time, but it must have been late in the evening, probably around ten or eleven at night. The harsh reality of life in this cell left little room for self-pity, yet my thoughts drifted to a rainy day from my childhood, a day that had brought both nostalgia and loneliness.

The rain had poured relentlessly outside my childhood home, and I couldn't help but feel a pang of longing for the days when I used to run and play with my friends in the neighborhood. The solitude in that jail cell made the memory all the more vivid and poignant. Before me, there were cucumber and squash plants, and in my boredom, I impulsively picked about ten of them. I broke three sticks and started crafting makeshift legs for the baby squash, creating a whimsical scene.

"Hey, you're ruining the squash! These are meant to be eaten, not played with!" A stern voice broke through my reverie, and I turned to see my grandmother scolding me. "Grandma, Grandma!" I yelled, but my voice fell on deaf ears. It was then that I woke up, my heart heavy with thoughts of my beloved grandmother.

My grandmother had passed away when I was just ten years old, leaving a void in my life that I had never truly filled. I wondered why she had scolded me in my dream. Was she displeased with my actions? My grandmother had raised five children, two boys and three girls. Tragically, my uncle Gani had lost his life in the war with the Nazis. This left my father as the only son in the family, with three sisters. One of my aunts lived in the city of Elbasan, another in the capital city of Tirana, and the eldest sister in a nearby village.

In her later years, my grandmother's health had deteriorated, and she relied on goods and better food that her daughters would send from the city of Elbasan. The bread in our village was subpar, and her daughter ensured she received fresh supplies every day by bus. I recalled one fateful day when she anxiously rose to check if her goods had arrived, only to fall and bruise herself badly. She was eighty-two years old at the time, and the fall left her chest bruised and caused severe diarrhea, leading to her passing in the midnight hours.

Chapter 12:

The Death of my Grandmother

I remember that somber night when my brothers and I shared a single bed. My mother's cries woke us from our slumber, and she begged us to get up. It was the night my grandmother had passed away. My father, who had been at the tavern, returned home and sobered up instantly. He instructed us to remain silent as he cleared the beds and placed my grandmother's lifeless body in the center of the room for viewing. I had never seen my father cry, but that night, he wept openly.

The funeral took place the same day, and I vividly remembered climbing up the hill to my neighbor's house, taking a shortcut from the funeral. As I walked, I thought about how I would share my experiences at a beautiful funeral, only to realize that the person being buried was my beloved grandmother. It was a moment of deep sadness, and I had nothing to share with anyone.

My grandmother had played a significant role in my life. She had provided for me, offered guidance, and cared for me in countless ways. She helped feed and clothe us, washed our clothes, and supported our family when my father's income often went to the tavern. Her pension, stemming from her loss during the war, was used to help us survive. Life in our family was already challenging under the communist regime, and my father's alcoholism only compounded our difficulties.

Over the years, I learned to put aside some of the pain and moved on to other aspects of life. However, thoughts of my grandmother would resurface from time to time. She had covered for me and taught me valuable life skills. My brother, the third child, had learned even more from her than I had. She was a wise woman, full of wisdom, grace, and love, and she had a profound impact on all of our lives. She was our guardian, and her passing left a void that could never be filled.

Seeing her in my dream brought back vivid memories, and I couldn't help but ponder the significance of her scolding me. It had been a long time since I had dreamt of her so vividly, and with plenty of time in my cell, I knew I would have the opportunity to reflect on those memories and their deeper meanings.

The morning had arrived, and I found myself on what I believed to be day seventeen of my time here. There were no pressing matters on my agenda, no appointments or tasks to complete within the confines of this prison facility. I rose from my bed and splashed some water on my face, feeling the weight of the days that had passed. As I caught my reflection in the metallic mirror, I couldn't help but pause and mutter to myself, "Still here."

My skin bore the marks of malnourishment and pallor, but my spirit remained unbroken. I had lost track of the time, but I returned to my bed, awaiting the arrival of breakfast. It was likely an hour or two away, and in that stillness, my mind drifted back to a memory of my uncle in Albania.

My uncle hailed from my mother's side of the family, and he was a young adult, possibly in his early twenties. He resided in the village of Sukth in Durrës, Albania, and would visit us a few times each year. His parents, my grandparents, had originally come from our village but had moved to Sukth in recent years. My grandfather was a skilled tradesman, renowned for his craftsmanship in building, and the "Gollobordo" valley, our region, was famed for its builders. Our people were masters of the trade, and many had migrated to other parts of Albania where their expertise was needed. However, the communist government strictly controlled one's place of residence, allowing migration only under certain conditions. Freedom to move was a rarity in communist Albania, as it allowed the government to maintain a tight grip on its citizens.

Sukth was situated between Tirana and Durrës, and to me, it was a place where my grandparents and my uncle resided, offering a warmer climate than our own unbearable village weather. Periodically, we would visit and stay with my uncle. On one such occasion, my uncle arrived at our house, and I inquired if I could accompany him to the village of Orzhanovce, which was approximately four hours' walk from our village.

During our journey, my uncle shared a story he had heard about a lady in the United States who had a regular job during her life but, upon her passing, was revealed to be a millionaire. He emphasized how even regular people in the U.S. had the opportunity to achieve success later in life due to the opportunities available in that country. He spoke of the freedom enjoyed in the United States, a place my mother often referred to as the "red apple," sparking my curiosity and admiration.

My uncle cautioned me not to share these thoughts with anyone due to the risk of arrest, but he wanted me to understand that there were better opportunities beyond the confines of Albania. His words left a lasting impression on me, and I kept his message to myself.

Our journey to the village was quite long, and I grew impatient, asking my uncle repeatedly when we would arrive. He playfully replied, "It's just over the hill," a phrase he repeated countless times, leading me to question whether we would ever reach our destination. My uncle had a mischievous sense of humor, and he enjoyed teasing me. We passed through another village where my uncle, instead of directly asking for food, approached a kind lady and told her that "the child" (referring to me) was hungry. The generous woman invited us in and offered bread and cheese before we continued on our way.

Upon arriving at the village of Orzhanovce, we were warmly welcomed by our relatives. In a room with no visible beds, I asked my uncle how we would sleep that night. He humorously pointed to some rolled-up mats made of bamboo-like wood behind the door and told me they would be our beds, standing upright. I was initially frightened at the prospect of sleeping in such a peculiar manner, but my uncle later revealed that it was all a joke. He had a penchant for teasing and would retell this humorous anecdote in the years that followed.

My uncle was a fun-loving individual with a unique perspective on life, and he had a close bond with me due to his rebellious spirit. Now, as I found myself far from home and uncertain about my future, I couldn't help but think of him and wonder if I would ever see him again.

I was jolted from my reverie as the door clanged open, signaling the arrival of tea, feta cheese, and French bread. Despite my hunger still gnawing at me, I relished this meager meal before returning to bed. I attempted to relax and uplift my spirits, knowing that the days here had to pass at some point. Yet, time seemed to stretch endlessly, making each moment feel like an eternity.

As I lay on my bed, my mind drifted back to a trip I had taken with my mother to Elbasan, Albania, when I was around twelve or thirteen years old. The journey from Klenje to Elbasan was arduous, with a treacherous road that wound through rugged terrain. Although the distance was only about 25 kilometers, the bus ride took approximately three hours. The landscape was characterized by steep mountains, winding paths, and treacherous descents, akin to the challenging camping areas I've encountered here in Idaho. The road was unpaved until the city of Librazhd, and it posed the constant risk of landslides as the bus traversed its uneven surface. At every turn, it felt as if we might tumble into the abyss below. To put it simply, it was far from a comfortable journey.

Our plan was to spend a day at my father's sister's house in Elbasan before continuing to my grandparents' home by train. The bus made a stop at the outskirts of Elbasan, a city that I wasn't very familiar with, and my knowledge of it was limited. However, as we disembarked onto the sidewalk, my eyes fell upon an ice cream truck. The images of the ice cream on display looked irresistibly delicious, and I longed for a taste. The price of an ice cream cone was seven Albanian leks, a sum my mother claimed she couldn't afford.

I became upset. We had traveled so far, and here we were in a different city, yet I couldn't even enjoy a simple ice cream. I knew that my mother kept her money secured tightly around her neck in a small pouch, and I seized it from her. With the baggy in my hands, I found twenty leks inside, enough to buy two ice creams—one for me and one for her. I relished the ice cream that day, and the memory remains vivid in my mind to this day. However, it was a bittersweet recollection, for I had resorted to stealing from my own mother to satisfy my craving. My mother had toiled tirelessly all day for minimal wages, and I had taken advantage of her to satisfy my desire for a simple pleasure. I later felt remorseful for my actions, but the memory lingered, and my mother recounted the story to everyone. It seemed like a tale to be retold with amusement, but the reality of that moment was far from enjoyable. I had literally torn the money pouch from her neck to obtain an ice cream. Ice cream had never been a common treat in our village. We endured harsh, cold weather, and no one produced or sold such luxuries. Life in Albania, particularly for the impoverished like us, was filled with hardships. I wished I could apologize to my mother for my actions, but now, in my current circumstances, I wondered if I would ever have the chance.

Feeling restless, I rose from my bed and began to pace. I had left behind my parents, my friends, and everything familiar to me. I had embarked on a journey into the unknown, uncertain of where it would lead, and the weight of my choices pressed heavily upon me. The cell's temperature had dipped, and I began to feel a chill creeping in. I reached for the thin blanket and tried to wrap it around myself as I lay on the bunk. While the blanket didn't provide much warmth, it at least offered the comfort of having something covering me. I lay on my left side, facing the bathroom stall, and my mind wandered back to a journey my mother and I had taken from Elbasan to the village where her parents lived.

The following morning, we had quite a walk ahead of us through Elbasan to reach the train station. It was my first encounter with a real train, something I had only read about in books until then. As we secured our tickets and boarded the train, I was struck by its noisy and somewhat dilapidated nature. Unlike the trains I had seen pictures the books, this one had ripped seats and was filled with passengers squeezed into a cramped space. I managed to secure a corner seat next to my mother, allowing me to gaze out of the window and take in the stunning Albanian landscape.

Albania was indeed a beautiful country. The scenery whizzed past the train, with everything close by appearing to speed by quickly, while objects in the distance seemed to slow down as we moved further away. It was an enjoyable journey, lasting approximately forty-five minutes to an hour, eventually taking us to the city of Durres. Durres was a captivating coastal city, known for its tourism due to the breathtaking beaches along the Adriatic Sea. The sand was soft, and the beaches stretched on for miles. I was enthralled by the city's architecture, and even many years later, I still vividly recall the beauty of Durres.

From Durres, we would continue our journey to Shijak and then Sukth via bus. My mother was the eldest daughter in her family, with my uncle being the only son, followed by two more daughters. One of my aunts lived nearby and had three children at the time, while the other aunt resided in the city of Tirana and had two boys. We often gathered with our cousins at our grandparents' home. However, I couldn't help but feel that we, the villagers, were treated differently. It seemed as though we were regarded with a certain condescension, likely due to the fact that we lived in the remote mountainous area and were not as frequently present around our grandparents as the other children were. I perceived a subtle bias, though I couldn't say for certain whether it was genuine or simply a product of my self-pitying view of our situation.

In those days, my younger aunt Lirije, or "the voice" as she was known, seemed to look down on us as mere villagers. At least, that's how I perceived it. Perhaps my judgment was clouded by my sense of our pitiable circumstances, but I always believed that my grandparents favored the other children because they spent more time with them. The shorter distance to travel made it easier for them to be at our grandparents' house, and they often visited at my uncle's invitation.

Chapter 13

Familial Struggles

During this period, I remembered that my younger aunt was going through a difficult time with her husband, who was dealing with mental health issues. Her life was marked by sadness, exacerbated by the tragic loss of her 10-year-old son, who had drowned in a pond near their home in Shijak. This loss had taken a toll on her husband's mental well-being, and he had become increasingly unstable. I witnessed the strain on my aunt as she grappled with her husband's deteriorating mental state and his abusive behavior.

To add to her struggles, both my uncle and grandparents pressured her to return to her husband, despite the abuse she endured. In Albania, even during the communist era, cultural norms and remnants of religious traditions exerted significant control over women's lives. Divorce was stigmatized, and women were expected to endure abusive marriages rather than leave their husbands. Albania was a country where women had few rights, and although the communist government preached equality, they often failed to protect women in abusive relationships. I couldn't help but hope for change and support for women like my aunt who faced such challenges, caught between the expectations of their families, societal norms, and their own difficult circumstances.

We stayed there for a whole week, seven days of pure delight. It was a precious opportunity for my mother to reunite with her parents and escape the relentless toil of our village life. As a family, along with our cousins, we embarked on a journey to explore the city of Durres. Wandering through the historic streets of old Durres, we reconnected with one another, creating cherished memories. One of the highlights of our trip was a visit to the beach. In Albania, beaches are places where people gather, bringing their umbrellas, towels, and forming groups to enjoy the sun, sea, and sand. At that time, I didn't know how to swim, so I cautiously ventured into the water, only going as far as I felt safe. It was my very first encounter with the sea, and its vastness intimidated me. I would wade in the water up to my waist, but venturing further felt unnerving.

In contrast, my uncle was a beach enthusiast. He had perfected the art of beach outings, bringing all the necessary supplies, including food, beer, salami, bread, and cheese, to create a splendid beachside feast. In my young mind, the taste of that beachfront lunch was nothing short of amazing. It wasn't that I had never tasted such foods before, but there was something magical about enjoying a meal at the seaside after a day of sun and sand. The flavors of olive oil, feta cheese, cucumbers, and tomatoes were heightened by the sea breeze, making every bite a delight.

For some reason, I often find myself reminiscing about those moments, trying to recreate that feeling of enjoying a delicious lunch with loved ones at the beach. You see, where I came from in the mountains, bodies of water were scarce, limited to small creeks. I recall a friend from the village who once jumped headfirst into a creek, only to emerge bloodied because it was far shallower than he had anticipated. Water bodies were unfamiliar territory for me. The sea, with its deep blue expanse and gentle ripples, was a marvel. I would lie in the sand, rolling it between my fingers, utterly captivated by this vast, otherworldly body of water. It felt like I was an alien discovering an entirely new world on Earth.

The beachgoers in Albania had a unique fashion sense, often sporting thin underpants, both men and women alike. This was a stark contrast to the conservative attire of our village. Visiting the beach and the city of Durres opened my eyes to a whole new world of experiences and possibilities. In our remote village, we were isolated, with only a select few having televisions. Those who did were typically party officials or those who could afford such luxuries. A television set cost a staggering 40,000 Albanian leks, equivalent to a year's salary for an official position. Most villagers had to choose between covering their daily expenses or saving up for a television, so only a fortunate few possessed this coveted device. While I had seen televisions, this was the first time I actually sat in front of one and watched its mesmerizing content.

Our days at the beach were followed by quality time spent with family, relishing the sweet grapes from the backyard. In the village where I grew up, grapes couldn't thrive due to the cold climate, so enjoying these exotic fruits at my grandparents' home was a treat. Moreover, the warmer weather allowed people to sleep with their doors open, a novel experience for me.

During our stay, my uncle and I bonded over conversations about the outside world. He had a unique profession as a TV repair specialist, and it was under his roof that I watched television for the very first time. Those days were filled with wonder as I discovered a world beyond the mountains and experienced things I had never seen before.

I rose from my bunk, feeling the need to use the toilet. After a brief stroll around the cell, I decided to do some pushups. In Albania, I had developed a fondness for pushups. I did them not only to build strength but also to alleviate the strain on my back, as I often found myself hunched over. It was a helpful practice.

I lowered myself to the floor and began my set of twenty pushups, feeling my breath shorten as the exercise progressed. After completing them, I stood up, slightly breathless, and sat back down on the bunk. As I gazed at the floor, my mind wandered back to a tragic event that had occurred one summer in our village – the passing of Silvana.

Chapter 14

The Tragic Tale of a Young Woman's Passing

Silvana's death had come suddenly, and she was just a teenager. To my knowledge, she had always been healthy. She was not only healthy but also extraordinarily beautiful. The stories circulating in the village suggested that her father had arranged her marriage to an older man who wasn't known for his intelligence. The reason behind this arrangement was the family's political connections and greater wealth, as they held better jobs and had influential connections.

Yet, Silvana had been in love with one of my cousins and friend, and they had spent countless hours together in the fields and hills surrounding our village. Their love story had become something of a legend among the villagers. They would often meet at night, and I had witnessed some of their clandestine encounters on the western side of the village, near the clinic and other spots. I even played a small role in delivering messages for them. Their love was deep and genuine.

However, my friend and his family didn't possess the reputation or future prospects that Silvana's father deemed suitable for his daughter, who was promised to another man. This decision deeply hurt my friend and many others in the village who cared for Silvana. The villagers viewed the man she was supposed to marry as utterly lacking in education and intelligence, akin to marrying a donkey. On the other hand, the man Silvana loved was good-looking, and they were genuinely compatible. They had shared their lives for a long time and were deeply in love. This story haunted our village for years, leaving an indelible mark due to the unjust and tragic ending of that innocent girl.

They lived at the outskirts of the village, not far from my house. After Silvana's death, her father locked himself away in their home. He turned to uncontrollable drinking and refused food and drink until the day he passed away. It may seem like an easy choice, but the pain of losing his daughter, a result of his own decision, tormented him. In Albania, autopsies were rarely performed, and medical professionals were scarce. No one investigated why someone would suddenly pass away. It has been suggested that Silvana might have chosen to poison herself rather than go through with the arranged marriage. The truth remains shrouded in mystery.

This tragic incident reflected a broader issue in communist Albania – parents decided who their children would marry, and marriages were often seen as unions between families, not just individuals. My friend, after Silvana's death, descended into a life of alcoholism for years. I hoped he would eventually find a way to heal and move forward. Silvana's absence left a void, and many nights, during my solitary missions on the government's side of town, I would visit her grave and share my thoughts, especially during those lonely hours when no one else was around. In times like those, when people could easily turn on each other for no apparent reason, I chose to go alone to avoid complications.

The sound of coughing from the neighboring room jolted me back to reality. I lowered my head, resting it on my knees, frozen in place, and utterly powerless. Time seemed to drag on relentlessly, and there was nothing I could do to hasten its passage.

Chapter 15

The Walnut Game

My mind wandered to memories of winters in our village, where work would come to a standstill. During those cold months, a cherished tradition united us as villagers. Behind a building situated to the southeast, known as the Cultural Center, we would gather. This building served as the repository for our musical instruments and traditional costumes, and it was a hub for various events, including dances, concerts, and political speeches. The person in charge happened to be a distant cousin of ours.

Just behind the Cultural Center, a walnut tree flourished, and the house of the tree's owner stood nearby. Walnuts held a special place in our village, not only as a source of sustenance but also for the games we played with them. One of the favorite winter pastimes was a game where we would gather and play with walnuts.

The game involved a nail and a coin, set up about ten feet away from a row of walnuts. The challenge was to knock the coin down using the walnuts, and whoever succeeded in this feat would collect all the walnuts involved. The victorious player could then sell them back to the others for money. By the end of the day, the person with the most walnuts had accumulated a small fortune, often amounting to two or three kilograms of these prized nuts to take home.

I would frequently observe this game, occasionally joining in the fun. The most skilled player in our village was a man named Sali, who happened to be my grandmother's nephew. He excelled at this game and was renowned throughout the village for his mastery. He was also entrusted with the role of the village night guard, patrolling with a vigilant eye and a firearm. Ironically, he was one of the people I aimed to avoid during my nightly endeavors. I would eagerly spend my hard-earned money on this game, despite the significant losses it incurred. It was undeniably entertaining, but it often resulted in a substantial dent in my savings. Regrettably, fights would occasionally erupt among those who had lost their life savings, unable to provide for their families due to the allure of this seemingly trivial game.

After the game, we would gather at the tavern, a place of congregation for both older and younger kids, though not always a harmonious one. It was here that we would socialize and unwind, a blend of camaraderie and tension lingering in the air.

I experienced a twinge of discomfort in my back while lying on the makeshift bed inside the cramped cell. This discomfort served as a reminder to get up and stretch, although time seemed to drag on endlessly in this dull and monotonous period of my life. The reoccurring though that I couldn't help but turn over and over was that I might never escape this place.

So, I settled back into my spot, placing my hand behind my head as I rested it on the pillow. Memories from my youth flooded my mind, like the time I had caught our neighbor's rooster and prepared it as a meal. Those were days of extreme poverty and malnourishment, and while I can't recall the exact age, I believe I was in my mid-teens.

Chapter 16

The Bold Feast: An Afternoon with the Rooster

One afternoon after returning from school, I found no one at home. Seizing the opportunity, I carefully lured the rooster into our house and swiftly prepared it for cooking. The neighborhood had a distinctive rooster, white with reddish plumage around the head, and it carried an air of confidence as it strutted through the area. This rooster was about a foot tall and remarkably healthy. It belonged to our neighbor to the southwest, who, in the days of old, had been the priest of the Serbian Orthodox Church in our village. Interestingly, our ancestry linked us as distant cousins.

During the time when the Turks had invaded Albania, many people converted from their native Orthodox faith to Islam. Our connection with the priest's family was a secretive one, as Theodore, the priest, continued to provide services in secret despite the religious restrictions in Albania. Worshipers operated covertly, and the Orthodox community in the village was known for their unity and resilience. Their heads were held low, and they remained vigilant because of Theodore's position as a priest, which often led to their families being stigmatized as "declassified" by the communist regime, signifying opposition.

On that fateful afternoon, I cooked the rooster, making sure to clean up thoroughly so that my family wouldn't suspect anything. After plucking the feathers and gutting it, I took the rooster with me, and together with a friend, we ventured into the mountains behind Osoi, specifically an area known as the Red Valley. This secluded spot, nestled behind picturesque mountains and ancient trees, offered an ideal location for our clandestine meal.

This meal was shared with my now-friend and cousin, who had once been a bully and had given me a hard time on many occasions. The old animosity between us had faded over time, replaced by mutual understanding. Together, we sat in the serene mountain setting, enjoying fresh rooster meat paired with generous amounts of alcohol. The air was filled with laughter and the warmth of newfound camaraderie, a stark contrast to the tension of the past.

We roasted the rooster over a fire we had built and toasted to the health of the rooster's owner for raising such a fine bird. These actions were born out of necessity, as meat and food were scarce, and each family had to find its own means of survival.

As we sat around the campfire, sipping on moonshine, we bonded and pledged to keep our secret tightly guarded. Later that evening, I learned that my neighbors were searching frantically for the missing rooster. However, I had covered my tracks effectively, and at that moment, I felt no guilt for taking it. Hunger and the scarcity of food at home had driven me to such actions. I did realize that someday, I might need to make amends for my actions, but for now, my primary concern was avoiding a seven-year prison sentence, something I was not willing to endure.

In this harsh reality of my country, I couldn't help but feel sadness and regret for what I had done to one of the most kind-hearted people in the neighborhood, someone who had always treated me with respect. Others considered me a foreign element in society, and it seemed only a matter of time before I ended up behind bars. This was the unfortunate reality of the place I called home.

My hands suddenly snapped back to reality, feeling numb as they rested beneath the pillow on my bed. The metal surface of the bed in the cell had always been uncomfortable, and I had never quite gotten used to it. The cell door swung open, and the guard delivered the usual meal - some meat, potatoes, and French bread. By now, I had consumed everything that came through that door, and yet, hunger still gnawed at my insides. Today, however, the guard had brought an extra piece of bread, a small gesture that brought a glimmer of comfort on this otherwise mundane night.

After finishing my meal, I reclined on the bed, and my mind drifted back to my earlier days when my older brother and I used to collect medicinal herbs. Among the six brothers in our family, he was the third, known for his intelligence and unwavering dedication to the family. He took on the role of a caretaker, especially when our father, who was a loving presence when sober, succumbed to alcoholism, leaving our mother in a state of abandonment.

Chapter 17

Fathers Glimpse of Sobriety

I cherished the memories of those sober mornings when my father and mother would discuss family matters, and he was truly the greatest person in the world during those moments. Our herbal collection efforts centered on juniper berries, which my father would later sell to the government, as there was a market for these berries. We would embark on day-long journeys without food or water, gathering juniper berries in a net made from cloth and oak tree branches. The bag would hang about half-full, and we'd use a stick to knock the juniper berries into the bag. Once the bag was full, we'd painstakingly remove the thorns and leaves, leaving behind only the beautiful black juniper berries.

Many people in our area engaged in this activity, so we had to venture into remote, mountainous regions to find untouched berry sources. Although I was no expert, I did my part, but my brother bore the brunt of the work. On our way up the mountain, he would grow tired, yet he always managed to outpace me, a source of irritation at the time. But as I reminisced, I remembered the hunger, the exhaustion, and my lack of energy during those days. This endeavor was not without its risks, as we encountered snakes and other wild animals that could have threatened our lives. Nevertheless, we persevered because our family relied on the financial support it provided, especially my mother, who worked long hours herding calves for the government.

When we returned home, there was no hot meal waiting for us. Instead, we scoured the garden for chicken eggs and fried them alongside a piece of tough cornbread that was hard to swallow. Despite the hardships, we took pride in our full bags, knowing that the money from the sale would soon follow. However, there were times when my father would sell the herbs and drink away the earnings, rendering our efforts seemingly futile in the end. Nonetheless, this experience instilled in me a strong work ethic and the valuable skill of working hard under any circumstances. The medicinal herb market did provide some additional income to the villagers who participated in it, although only a few families were involved. If everyone had taken part, finding juniper and other medicinal herbs would have become increasingly difficult. Although I never knew precisely what the government did with these herbs, I had heard that they were used to create medicine or support the health and well-being of the people in communist Albania.

Chapter 18

The Beating

I tossed and turned on the bunk bed, struggling to find a comfortable position for rest. The day had been exceptionally beautiful in the city of "Shkozeet." As I walked between the school and the mess hall, heading west to the gate after school, I couldn't help but notice the picturesque surroundings. Beyond the gate, there was a dirt path that stretched horizontally, leading me into a vast, lush cornfield. The corn stood tall and vibrant green as I ventured into its midst.

Suddenly, I found myself ambushed by three men. They had a vaguely familiar appearance, though not entirely recognizable. They forcibly dragged me into the cornfield and stripped me naked before carrying me to an area where a power pole with a triangular, metallic high-tension power ball stood. I lay on the ground, defenseless, as one of the men named Xhike dropped a snake onto me. The snake slithered across my left leg, up my chest, and over my other shoulder. Panic consumed me, and I began yelling for help until I abruptly woke up.

The sound of a guard checking on me reassured me that it had all been a dream. I had been gripped by fear and confusion as I got up, realizing that the place seemed eerily familiar. While I couldn't make sense of the snake, I did understand that I had endured a brutal beating in that field, involving these three men. This wasn't a mere tale; it was a painful memory etched into my past.

One of the individuals, whose name escaped me, was Xhike. He was tall with brown hair, lean and agile. He possessed a skill for combat, and I must have been around fifteen or sixteen when this incident occurred during my time at the agricultural mechanical school. It all began with an innocently joking comment I made at my cousin's home, where this guy had recently been released from an Albanian prison. It was akin to the "pick up the soap" joke in the United States, but it had severe consequences for me. Xhike punched me in the gut, leaving me gasping for air, then struck me in the head. Before long, I found myself stripped naked and subjected to relentless punches and kicks. He even took a cigarette and burned it onto my foot, causing excruciating pain. This torment seemed to last an eternity, and I genuinely feared for my life. Yet, miraculously, I survived.

I reported the incident to the school, which involved the police. I was subsequently taken to the hospital, where they determined that the beating had caused my kidneys to produce blood in my urine. It was an experience that haunted me, replaying in my mind over and over again. My anger and desire for revenge simmered within me, but I was pressured by the gang not to press charges, as it could have had deadly consequences.

Ultimately, I left the school and returned to my village, a decision that, in hindsight, may have been the best for my safety at the time. It became apparent that I had very little understanding of the world and its complexities, unable to distinguish between seemingly good and bad individuals. The dream had resurfaced these painful memories, leaving me overwhelmed with sadness and helplessness.

During my time in the hospital, an older man had also tried to harm me, prompting me to flee the hospital and return to school. A few days later, I was permitted to return home to the village, likely due to my father's connections and standing in the community. Although my father lacked financial means, his extensive connections, earned through his role in managing the supply chain, held significant influence with the communist authorities.

As I sat on the bed, the memories and the dream weighed heavily on my mind. Life had been exceptionally tough in Albania, a place where it often felt that no one could genuinely protect you. Yet, in moments of despair, I couldn't help but believe that perhaps some higher power had watched over us, and for that, I remained deeply grateful. I returned to the bunk bed and lay down. Turning onto my right shoulder, I gazed at the wall, attempting to fall asleep once more, but sleep eluded me. My eyes fixated on the pattern of the bricks, and I found myself drifting back to my childhood.

Back then, as darkness fell, I would venture into the bushes behind my house, clutching a bottle of wine. It was my time, a moment of solace, where I could slip away into the night and concoct plans for the evening's activities. The town's center was no longer the focal point; instead, it was the hidden nooks in the surrounding bushes. There, I would acquire items from the government that I could sell, all without ever bringing anything home to my parents. I feared implicating them in my activities, as I knew I was solely responsible for my actions.

Those were the times when I would scout the area for opportunities, eavesdropping on hushed conversations that others believed were private. I couldn't help myself; I remained concealed and listened attentively. As a result, I became privy to numerous secret stories within the village, although I never shared that information with anyone. It merely acquainted me with the villagers and their myriad problems. I would sit in the grass at night, contemplating various aspects of life. In fact, those were some of the most enjoyable days of my life. Lost in my thoughts, I would ponder marriage and my future, envisioning a life outside of Albania. Yet, I was well aware that such dreams and aspirations were virtually unattainable in Albania, where the government held a tight grip on individuals, dictating their destinies.

Nevertheless, I dreamt big, aspiring to wield power like the communist leaders. They had wives and mistresses, and the government turned a blind eye to such matters. As I lay in the grass and gazed at the sky, I marveled at the vivid image of the Milky Way and thousands of beautiful stars. In my village, with the pitch-black surroundings, the sky seemed boundless. I would gaze at the stars, including Polaris, and wonder if there were any other beings out there and how distant they might be. The heavens appeared simultaneously beautiful and daunting.

Contemplating my future, I couldn't envision where I would be in thirty-five years. There was nothing in my mind to paint a picture of what I truly desired. I harbored a profound fear of the government, yet I remained determined to break any rules I could evade. It was simply who I was. I refused to conform to the ideology imposed upon me, even though my family's welfare weighed heavily on my mind. I often wondered what would become of them if I were to escape. Those days of roaming the village, exploring the bushes and fertile grasslands, held a unique beauty. I continually reshaped myself intellectually, often creating mental environments where I held control, where safety and prosperity reigned. I derived immense pleasure from these mental constructs. I would close my eyes and immerse myself in dream scenarios where I wielded power, helped others, and improved the lives of my family. It was my sanctuary; a place that made me feel worthy and motivated to do whatever was necessary to survive.

Chapter 19

Scenes of Beyond in the dark

One unsettling reality in the village was the prevalence of infidelity, hidden under the cover of darkness amidst the cornfields and grasslands. I became aware of numerous extramarital encounters. It was an unspoken truth, a phenomenon where individuals cheated on their spouses while denying any wrongdoing. Even those who were married would engage in these affairs, only to later carry on as if nothing had happened. It was a despicable aspect of the system, and I found myself experiencing and witnessing these events firsthand. It led me to conclude that communism was a sham, a system riddled with hypocrisy and moral decay.

The passage of time in the Macedonian prison seemed to drag along at a snail's pace. However, with only a few days left until my release, my anxiety began to mount. I couldn't help but wonder about what lay ahead for me. The rumor mill had it that I was to be sent to a United Nations camp in Belgrade, Serbia. In those final days, I found myself growing increasingly fidgety and unsettled.

Sitting on my bunk bed, I couldn't help but reminisce about the day I had escaped my homeland. Escaping Albania had been a harrowing and nerve-wracking experience. I vividly remembered hearing stories of people being killed at the border, and within our borders, only one person had ever successfully escaped before—a fellow from a nearby village who had been living in Tirana, the capital city. Others who had attempted to flee had met with tragic ends at the border.

On that day, my emotions were in turmoil as I watched my mother diligently bending over, washing our clothes. The journey to the border was a forty-five-minute walk, leading through woods, basins, and alongside a creek flowing down from the mountains. Some sections of the path featured red soil, which had been worn down by countless footfalls over time. These were once horse trails, and no cars could traverse these rugged routes.

My emotions were a whirlwind, and I found myself thinking about a myriad of topics—people, situations, friends, and more. As I drew closer to my destination, I suddenly came across a snake in the middle of the road. I cannot describe the exact species, but my innate fear of snakes typically led me to try and kill them. However, on this day, something was different. I simply let the snake continue on its way, heading uphill just like me. For some reason, I felt that today was not its day to die. In that moment, I began pondering the role of animals on Earth and their place in the world. It was an unusual day, and it seemed that my actions were changing me in unexpected ways, filling me with empathy for other creatures.

Perhaps it was the anticipation of freedom that made me want to grant the snake its own taste of liberty. I found myself shaking my head in amazement, wondering why I had thought about such things on that particular day. It was as though, deep down, I felt that my imprisonment was coming to an end, and that a new chapter awaited me—one filled with hope and change.

Walking along the road with the snake by my side, I was surrounded by towering fir trees, their branches forming a canopy that shielded me from the sun's harsh rays. The gentle breeze brushed against my face and hair, making it a truly memorable day. It wasn't an ordinary, mundane day; it was a day filled with the potential for transformative ideas, thoughts, and actions.

My mind kept returning to the decision I had made—to embark on this journey of change, even though I had no idea where it would lead. Despite the uncertainty, there was a persistent feeling within me that assured me I would be okay. I recalled my grandmother's unwavering faith in God, and even though I had questioned it as a child, at that moment, I felt guided by something, a sense of change on the horizon.

And indeed, change did come. I was no longer in Albania, and my life was set on a new course—a path toward a better future. Slowly, I became convinced that my time in the Macedonian prison had been the price I paid for my daring escape from Albania. Just as these thoughts swirled in my mind, the prison door swung open, and the guard brought another meal.

Lunchtime had arrived, and our meal consisted of a can of spam and some bread. My hunger overpowered my distaste for spam, and I proceeded to prepare my sandwich by breaking the bread in half and spreading the spam onto it with a plastic knife. It wasn't a culinary delight, but it served as a source of sustenance rather than a gourmet treat.

As I sat on the bunk in the prison cell, my mind wandered back to a particular day in my past. It was the day I had brought a goat home to our family behind our village, nestled in the western part of our town, near an area known as the "livada."

I recalled the circumstances vividly. I had been roaming around, and for some reason, I found myself observing a herd of goats making their way back to the government barns in the northeastern part of the town. One man was herding around 200 goats, leading them down from the mountains to the barns.

In a spontaneous and daring moment, I decided to grab one of the goats by its horns and lead it into a dark tunnel. There, I waited until it was pitch dark outside. With my shirt wrapped around the goat's mouth and horns to muffle its sounds, I remained hidden in the tunnel. These tunnels, meant for shelter in case of bombings, weren't the safe havens one might imagine. They were dark and damp, and the experience was far from pleasant.

Once night had fully fallen, I emerged from the pitch-black tunnel and wrestled with the massive goat, probably weighing around 250 lbs. I managed to lead it from its hiding place through a small creek near our house and into our barn. It was no small feat, and by the time I got home, I was quite flustered. I immediately sought out my father and urgently told him that he needed to come with me. He asked what the matter was, and I explained that he had to come home with me right away because it was an emergency. Together, we went to the barn, and I requested that he butcher the goat immediately. My father was skilled in the art of butchering, having experience with lamb and cows, and he possessed a trusty knife.

I told him in no uncertain terms that I could not afford to be caught and sent to prison, so he had to act swiftly. Thankfully, my father complied, and we had meat for the winter ahead. My mother expertly salted the meat to preserve it, and nobody ever discovered that the goat had gone missing. It was a challenging decision to make and execute, but it ensured that we had food for the winter without arousing suspicion from the government.

I rose from my bunk and began pacing around the cell, feeling the sluggish passage of time. It brought to mind memories of my mother, who had been quite the storyteller in her own right. We used to gather around her, whether we were working on separating healthy juniper berries from the unhealthy ones, or during special occasions and holidays, like the ones when we'd form a circle in the room and listen to her enchanting tales from the past.

My mother possessed a remarkable storytelling skill, and when she wove her stories, it created the most delightful evenings our family had ever known. During these events, she would prepare delicious pita and baklava, enticing all of us to participate and come together as a family. Her repertoire of fairy tales was extensive, akin to the ones one might find in modern United States, with princesses, Cinderella, and Snow White. These storytelling sessions were among the most cherished experiences of my life.

In our modest home, we had a small radio, and it played beautiful folk music from Macedonia, as my village was located near the Macedonian border, and the primary language spoken was Macedonian or Bulgarian, rather than Albanian. The music added a rich layer to our cultural heritage and the childhood she had grown up with. My mother was a victim of an arranged marriage, a common practice in our community. However, some of us, including myself, held more liberal views. She would occasionally share her own love stories from her past, which contrasted with the arranged marriage that had bound her to my father.

Despite the circumstances, our mother loved and cared for us with a depth and dedication that only a parent could provide. Her warmth and resilience became the foundation of our lives, even as we faced relentless hardship. My father, however, was often absent, lost in his struggles with alcoholism. His absence left a void that my mother worked tirelessly to fill, her strength a quiet force holding us together. I often thought about those mesmerizing fairy tales she used to tell us. Her voice had the power to transport us to magical worlds, far removed from our reality. I wished I could spin stories with the same beauty and wonder as she did.

By this time, the longing for my family had grown into an ache that consumed me. A maelstrom of emotions churned within me—a relentless mix of fear, sadness, and longing. On one hand, there was the haunting fear that I might never see my loved ones again. On the other, a fragile hope glimmered in the distance, whispering that at least I was moving forward, however uncertainly. This fragile balance was compounded by the grim reality of my situation: trapped within the walls of Macedonia's state prison, I wrestled with the belief that freedom might remain forever out of reach.

Isolation pressed down on me, heavy and suffocating. The thought of being utterly alone, abandoned in a world that seemed indifferent to my struggles, seeped into my very core. Anxiety gnawed at me constantly. Questions swirled in my mind, unrelenting and unanswerable. How would I fend for myself once released? How could I adapt to this unfamiliar culture, to these people whose lives I didn't understand? I had no guide, no financial safety net, no clear direction to follow. The sheer weight of the unknown was enough to crush anyone's spirit.

But in the face of this uncertainty, one thing remained unwavering: there was no turning back. The decision to cross the border had been made, and it was final. The life I had left behind in Albania was no longer an option. The road ahead, though shrouded in mystery, was now my only path. Each step forward felt like both a triumph and a test of courage. Even though I was adrift in a sea of uncertainty, there was an undeniable strength in choosing to move forward.

This journey, fraught with fear, determination, and resilience—was not just about finding freedom. It was about discovering the depths of my own spirit and the courage to embrace an unknown future. While the destination was still undefined, the resolve to face whatever lay ahead burned brighter than the doubt. Hope, fragile yet steadfast, was the force that carried me forward.

Chapter 20

Seeking Refuge

Information had been scarce until recent days when I received word of acceptance by the United Nations High Commissioner for Refugees (UNHCR), granting me refugee status. This revelation was both comforting and terrifying. While it offered a glimmer of hope, the reality of being a refugee, a term previously associated only with distant conflicts, now loomed large before me.

As the days in captivity dwindled, preparations for my release commenced. Summoned one morning, I gathered my few belongings, marking the end of my thirty-day ordeal. Nicola, the familiar interrogator, delivered the news of my imminent relocation to Padinska Skela, Belgrade, Yugoslavia, and the uncertain prospects that lay beyond. His parting words echoed a strange mix of admonition and solicitude, urging me to remember Macedonia fondly and offering a lifeline should I ever need assistance.

Standing before him, a profound sense of desolation washed over me. The scars of physical and emotional torment bore witness to the harrowing journey that had brought me to this juncture. Any semblance of excitement had long been supplanted by a pervasive fear of the unknown. Awaiting transport to the bus station, I found myself in a daze, surveying the stark surroundings with detached resignation. The person who had entered Albania was no more; in his place stood a hardened survivor, burdened by self-pity, pain, and the weight of newfound responsibilities.

As I contemplated the uncertain path ahead, a guard interrupted my reverie, signaling the moment to depart. With little more than a small bag in tow, I left behind the only semblance of comfort—a blanket discarded in the prison. Yet, its absence failed to register amidst the urgency to move forward. Stepping into a nondescript green SUV, I took one last look at the prison's imposing facade. As the vehicle merged into traffic, a sense of liberation washed over me. For the first time in what felt like an eternity, I breathed in the crisp air of freedom, unshackled by chains or constraints. Though escorted by security agents, the absence of restraints marked a symbolic shift—a tentative step towards an uncertain future, wherever it may lead.

As I settled into the back seat of the SUV, the driver informed me that we were en route to the bus station in Niš, Serbia. Leaving behind the bustling cityscape of Skopje, the capital of North Macedonia, we embarked on a journey that promised a blend of natural beauty and cultural richness. Our path unfolded along a well-maintained highway that wound its way through a diverse landscape. Initially, we passed through verdant valleys adorned with picturesque villages and expanses of fertile farmland. Fields of golden wheat swayed in the gentle breeze, while vibrant sunflowers turned their faces toward the sun, painting the countryside with bursts of color.

As we journeyed onward, the terrain gradually transitioned, with the highway ascending into hilly landscapes. Serpentine roads offered sweeping views of the surrounding countryside, punctuated by occasional rest stops where travelers could pause and admire the scenery. Along the route, quaint towns and hamlets provided glimpses into the rural charm of the region.

Entering Serbia, the road widened, affording smoother travel through vast expanses of agricultural land. Fields of corn, sunflowers, and wheat stretched to the horizon, framed by distant hills adorned with patches of dense forest. As we neared Niš, the scenery grew more rugged, with rocky outcrops and ancient fortresses dotting the landscape. Historic landmarks hinted at the region's rich cultural heritage, weaving a tapestry of stories from centuries past. Finally, the road broadened into a bustling thoroughfare as we approached Niš. Modern infrastructure blended harmoniously with centuries-old architecture, offering a glimpse into the vibrant Serbian life.

In essence, the journey from Skopje to Niš unfolded like a tale of two worlds, each offering its own unique charm and allure. From the tranquility of rural landscapes to the vibrant pulse of city life, the road beckoned travelers to discover the natural beauty and cultural richness that lay along its path.

During my journey, the security officers accompanying me shared an abundance of information, attempting to shed light on the nature of my upcoming destination, Padinska Skela, a temporary holding facility en route to refugee accommodations in Belgrade. Amidst this exchange, a mixture of genuine insight and potential misinformation unfolded, providing me with a curious glimpse into the perspectives and prejudices of those around me.

As we traversed the road, conversations ebbed and flowed between the officers, revealing underlying tensions and biases. It became evident that there was a palpable disdain towards Kosovo and the Albanian population residing within Macedonia, referred to derogatorily as "Skiptari," in contrast to the term "Albanci" used for Albanians from Albania proper. While I strained to grasp the nuances of their discourse, I was acutely aware of the historical animosity between Slavic Macedonians and Albanians, perpetuated by political propaganda espoused by figures like Enver Hoxha.

Despite the mutual antipathy between Macedonians and Albanians, I found myself in a unique position as an outsider from Albania proper. This distinction afforded me a certain detachment from the tensions simmering beneath the surface, allowing me to observe with a mixture of curiosity and trepidation. It was a revelation of sorts, providing me with invaluable insights into the complexities of interethnic relations in the region and offering a glimpse into the challenges that lay ahead.

Upon our arrival at the bus station in Niš, Serbia, I was greeted by a spectacle of movement and noise that epitomized the essence of travel. The station loomed large against the cityscape of Niš, a testament to modernity with hints of tradition woven into its architectural design. As I stepped inside, I was enveloped by a whirlwind of activity, the air buzzing with the chatter of travelers and the rumble of departing buses. The main concourse served as the beating heart of the station, a bustling thoroughfare lined with ticket counters, cafes, and information desks. Here, travelers congregated, clutching their tickets and luggage, as they prepared to embark on their respective journeys. The aroma of freshly brewed coffee mingled with the scent of baked goods, creating an atmosphere of warmth and familiarity amidst the hustle and bustle.

Surrounding the concourse, platforms bustled with activity as buses arrived and departed in a choreographed dance of motion. Luggage carts rumbled along the platforms, ferrying passengers' belongings to and from, while travelers hurried to locate their designated coaches amidst the sea of vehicles. Despite the chaos, there was a semblance of order, a rhythm that pulsed through the station with the precision of a well-oiled machine.

Beyond the main concourse, a labyrinth of corridors and passageways beckoned, leading to various amenities and services. From restrooms and waiting lounges to snack bars and souvenir shops, the station offered everything a weary traveler could desire. Venturing outside, the station opened onto a bustling plaza, where taxis and tuk-tuks vied for space amidst a throng of pedestrians. Vendors peddled their wares from makeshift stalls, while street performers entertained passersby with their music and dance.

Amidst the hum of voices, the shuffle of hurried feet, and the strains of folk music filling the air, the bus station in Niš, Serbia, pulsed with life. It wasn't just a place of transit—it was a living, breathing reflection of Serbia's soul, a space where people from all walks of life converged. Travelers, young and old, hurried across platforms, their faces a mosaic of emotions: anticipation, weariness, joy. Vendors shouted their wares, children clung to parents, and announcements echoed overhead in Serbian, painting a portrait of a nation alive with motion.

This place, with its vibrant energy and constant rhythm, was more than a mere station. It was a testament to connection—a bridge where past and present intertwined seamlessly. Here, amidst the chaos and order, the resilience of the Serbian spirit was palpable.

As I stood amidst the throng, a familiar melody wafted through the air, halting me in my tracks. The strains of Serbian folk music transported me back to another time, another place. Suddenly, I was a child again in Albania, sitting beside my family as we huddled in secret, listening to the forbidden notes of *Pozdravje*. Those melodies, carried across the airwaves despite the Communist regime's best efforts to silence them, became our lifeline.

We would gather on Albanian beaches, hidden from the prying eyes of government informants, clutching tiny, smuggled radios. There, amidst the golden sands and the rhythmic crash of waves, we found our freedom. The music flowed over us like a balm, soothing the wounds of a repressive existence. For those brief moments, the world beyond Albania's borders didn't feel so far away.

The Albanian government saw music not as art, but as rebellion. To them, the notes of foreign songs were a dangerous spark, capable of igniting dreams of freedom. They erected signal blockers to drown out Yugoslavian broadcasts and meted out harsh punishments to those who dared to listen. A single note from beyond the border could result in a seven-year prison sentence, branding the listener a traitor for indulging in what they called "foreign elements." But no amount of fear could extinguish the human spirit. Serbian music seeped into Albania like sunlight through cracks in a wall, defying every effort to block it. For my family, and countless others, these songs weren't just rebellion—they were survival. The heartfelt lyrics and soothing rhythms reminded us of a world filled with beauty and possibility, even in the face of relentless oppression.

My uncle—my mother's brother—was our unsung hero in this silent resistance. A skilled TV repairman, he turned his expertise into a tool for defiance. Under the cover of night, he built makeshift antennas to intercept Yugoslavian broadcasts. Through his ingenuity, forbidden melodies and television programs entered our home, filling the silence with hope.

But secrecy was our lifeline. The moment someone knocked on the door, radios were silenced, televisions switched off, and the house became a picture of compliance. Paranoia ran deep; neighbors, colleagues, even family members could be informants. The regime's power lay not only in its control but in its ability to sow distrust. Families were fractured by suspicion, love overshadowed by fear. Through it all, my uncle's quiet defiance became a beacon. To him, bringing music into our lives wasn't just about sound—it was about preserving humanity in a world that sought to erase it. Each forbidden note was a reminder that beauty could thrive even in darkness. Those melodies became lifelines, binding us to a world beyond our isolation and whispering of a freedom we could only dream of.

Standing in the Niš bus station, those memories washed over me. The same melodies that once carried so much risk now played freely, echoing in their homeland without fear. The warmth of those notes, the courage they represented, and the resilience they inspired filled my heart with gratitude. Serbia's music, like its people, was beautiful—its harmonies a testament to the unyielding strength of the human spirit, its rhythms a celebration of freedom.

As I stood lost in thought, a security officer approached me, holding out a cone of vanilla ice cream. The simple gesture caught me off guard—a small act of kindness that felt profound. As I savored the creamy sweetness, the unexpected generosity reminded me of the goodness in the world. It was a stark contrast to the paranoia I had grown up with, a symbol of the trust and humanity that still thrived here.

The bus ride to Belgrade was unlike anything I had ever experienced. The bus itself was a marvel: plush, comfortable seats upholstered in blue-gray fabric, offering a level of luxury I had never known. The vehicles I had grown up with in Albania were rugged and unforgiving, with cracked leather seats and jarring rides. This was different. Settling into my seat, I felt as though I were stepping into a new world, a world of ease and possibility. As the bus rumbled out of Niš, the Serbian countryside unfolded like a masterpiece painting. Rolling hills stretched into the horizon, their vibrant greens shimmering under the sunlight. Fields of wildflowers added bursts of color, while the distant mountains stood like guardians, timeless and steady. The trees lining the highway swayed gently in the breeze, their leaves whispering secrets of the land's resilience.

Each mile felt like shedding another layer of my past—the fear, the repression, the weight of survival. The landscape filled me with a sense of awe and possibility. I wasn't just traveling to Belgrade; I was moving toward a future that felt open and full of promise. This wasn't merely a journey; it was a **rebirth**. The music, the kindness of strangers, and the beauty of Serbia reminded me of the resilience that had carried me through the darkest times. They showed me that even after years of silence, joy could return, and hope could thrive. With each passing mile, I left behind the shadows of my past and stepped into a brighter, freer world. In that moment, I knew—everything was going to be okay.

Chapter 21

Reflections from the Past

Memories flooded my mind as I gazed out at the passing scenery, transporting me back to a time long ago. I remembered the treacherous bus rides of my childhood, particularly one journey from Klenja to Elbasan that had left a lasting impression on me. The unpaved roads, perilously close to steep cliffs, had filled me with a sense of dread, as if at any moment we might plunge into the abyss below.

One memory stood out vividly in my mind—a tragic incident that had occurred on a similar bus journey years ago. A sick man, the father of my childhood friends, had been traveling to the city of Librazhd in search of medical help. Half an hour before reaching his destination, I heard the frantic shouts from the back of the bus as he took his last breath, succumbing to kidney failure. The scene had left me shaken, a stark reminder of the harsh realities of life in Albania, where access to medical care was limited and death often came swiftly and unexpectedly.

As I reflected on these memories, a surge of emotion washed over me—anger at the communist government that had brought such suffering upon its people, and determination to seek a better life beyond the borders of my homeland. In Belgrade, I hoped to find refuge from the hardships of life in Albania, to build a future free from the constraints of poverty and oppression.

As the bus rumbled onwards towards Belgrade, the landscape outside the window unfolded with mesmerizing detail, each passing scene adding depth to the journey ahead. The road stretched out before us, an endless ribbon of asphalt cutting through the rugged terrain of Serbia. Approaching Aleksinac, a town thirty-five to forty kilometers north of Niš, the landscape transformed dramatically. The outskirts revealed a mix of modern structures and historic buildings, each telling stories of the town's rich heritage. Landmarks stood out, from ancient ruins to medieval fortifications, offering glimpses into Aleksinac's storied past. Yet, the town was not just a relic of history—it thrived as an industrial hub, with factories and chimneys symbolizing economic vitality in manufacturing and mining.

As the bus rolled through its streets, Aleksinac's resilience and vibrancy were palpable. The town blended tradition and progress, reflecting the indomitable spirit of its people. Even as we left Aleksinac and continued toward Belgrade, its memory lingered—a microcosm of Serbia's past, present, and future, where history and modernity converged to shape its destiny with courage and determination.

Sitting to my left on the bus was a tall, wiry man with a square face and neatly combed hair that swooped to the right. Something about his appearance pulled me back in time, reminding me of Doula, the vice principal and math teacher from my school days in Albania. Doula wasn't just a teacher—he was a distant cousin of my father's and a staunch supporter of the Communist regime. His influence was everywhere, hovering over us like a dark cloud, dictating how we should live, speak, and even think. It was one of those dreadful nights when fate and fury collided. I had been suspended from school, my frustration with the system bubbling over. That evening, I went to the local tavern to meet friends, trying to escape the weight of it all. As we smoked and mingled, there he appeared—Doula. His presence turned the air heavy, and his words sliced through the camaraderie like a blade.

"You're just another smoker, a drinker," he said, loud enough for everyone to hear. "Exactly what the foreign elements want you to become."

His tone was belittling, laced with the superiority of a man who thrived on control. Something snapped in me at that moment. My suspension, his judgment, the oppressive weight of Albania's rigid society—it all boiled over. I stood up, my voice shaking with anger.

"I'm finished with school!" I shouted. "You suspended me, so I don't care who you are or what you say."

Before I knew it, my hand reached for the nearest object—an ashtray. Without thinking, I hurled it at his head. The tavern fell silent, the moment hanging heavy in the air.

Doula's reaction was swift and brutal. He lunged at me, his hand cracking across my face with a force that sent stars exploding before my eyes. Twice, three times, his palm struck me, leaving my head ringing. Pain radiated through my skull as humiliation and rage churned in my chest. I staggered, desperate to retaliate, reaching for anything within arm's length. But before I could strike again, my friends dragged me outside, their hands gripping my shoulders as I fumed with fury.

That night, my head throbbed with more than just physical pain. It was the kind of ache that came from helplessness, from realizing how deeply embedded the system was in our lives. Doula wasn't even my teacher anymore, yet he had the power to beat me in public, unchecked and unchallenged.

The next morning, the full weight of the system bore down on me. I was summoned to the office of the party secretary room that reeked of fear and authority. He leaned over his desk, his voice low but menacing.

"If you don't learn to respect the community and its teachers," he warned, "you'll be sent away for life."

Sent away for life. The words echoed in my head like a death sentence. I knew what they meant. The Communist regime had no room for dissent, no patience for those who didn't conform. That day, my hatred for Albania's oppressive government and its enforcers solidified. They weren't just people—they were extensions of a machine that crushed individuality and freedom under its heel.

That night, I was taken home. My head still ached, my thoughts spinning. I stared at the ceiling, my mind a blur of anger, fear, and determination. I swore to myself that I would not let this system define me, even if it meant leaving everything behind.

The memory clung to me as I sat on the bus, the man on my left oblivious to the turmoil his appearance had stirred. I turned my gaze to the window, watching the Serbian countryside roll by. The hills and fields outside were a world apart from those stifling days in Albania. The open landscape felt like a reflection of my own journey—away from control, away from fear, and toward a future that I hoped would be free.

Though my headache had faded, the memory of that night lingered, a painful reminder of what I had escaped and why I could never go back. The ache wasn't just in my head anymore; it was a part of me, etched into my being. And as the bus rumbled forward, I shook off the memory like dust from my shoulders, determined to focus on the promise of what lay ahead.

Continuing along the highway, Paracin came into view, a dynamic blend of industry and agriculture. The town center's cobblestone streets, lined with vibrant, intricately detailed buildings, exuded a timeless charm. The Church of St. Nicholas stood out with its striking Serbian Orthodox architecture, its domed roof reaching skyward, and its interior frescoes depicting biblical scenes, reflecting deep spiritual roots.

Paracin's thriving industrial sector added a modern energy, with factories and warehouses bustling with activity, underscoring its role as a regional economic hub. This unique interplay of history and progress left a lasting impression, showcasing the harmony of tradition and vitality in Serbia's cultural and economic fabric.

My head turned inward as the bus rumbled on, my gaze settling on the faces of the other passengers. Each expression told its own quiet story, some weary, some hopeful, others unreadable. Watching them stirred something deep within me, memories rising unbidden like ghosts from the past. In that moment, as I looked around, I remembered my father.

It was just two months before my escape when my brother Shaq and I decided to visit him in the city of Bulqiza. My father had been incarcerated for an indeterminate length of time, and the journey to see him was arduous. For hours, we walked through the rugged mountains, our footsteps crunching against the rocky trails.

Somewhere along the way, we stopped to rest on a grassy slope, the kind of peaceful spot that might make you forget the weight of the world for a while. We consumed snacks we had brought, and I lay back on the cool grass, staring up at the vast, open sky. From where we rested, the mountains stretched out toward Yugoslavia, their peaks a silent invitation to the world beyond.

I didn't realize what I was saying as I spoke to my brother, my thoughts flowing freely in the stillness of that moment. "I wonder what's beyond those mountains," I murmured, more to myself than to him.

Shaq turned to me sharply, his disapproval written all over his face. "I know what you're thinking," he said, his voice low and stern. "You're thinking about crossing the border, aren't you?"

I looked at him and smiled, trying to brush off his suspicion with feigned innocence. "Oh no," I replied". "I would never leave you behind."

Even as the words left my mouth, I felt their hollowness. Deep down, I knew what I was contemplating, but such thoughts were dangerous—treasonous even. If Shaq had chosen to report me, the consequences would have been unthinkable. Yet, in that fragile moment, he didn't press further, and we continued our journey.

When we finally reached the prison, my heart sank at the sight of my father. Once a man of vitality and strength, he now stood before us in a pale-yellow jumpsuit, his skin ashen, his spirit diminished. He was no longer the father I remembered, the one who had once navigated the complexities of life with resourcefulness and resolve.

Before his imprisonment, my father had been a man of many roles. He had worked as a bartender, then climbed his way up to become a controller of the supply chain, a position that required him to deal with Communist officials—the so-called bigwigs. He had always been resourceful, making sure the system's demands were met while providing for his family. But that resourcefulness had become his undoing.

The same people he served—the officials he had supplied and catered to—turned on him. They swindled him, twisting the truth to create a deficit in the supply chain and pinning the blame on him. The hypocrisy of it all stung deeply. These were the people who would shake your hand by day and stab you in the back by night, all while spouting the ideals of Communist unity.

Seeing my father in that state broke something inside me. The man I had admired, who had once seemed unshakable, was now reduced to a shadow of himself. The memory haunted me for days, his pale face and sunken eyes a constant reminder of how easily the system could crush even the strongest among us.

The Communist regime wasn't just a government, it was a mafia. It demanded compliance, loyalty, and absolute submission, and it punished anyone who dared to deviate. My father's imprisonment was proof of how unforgiving and hypocritical the system was. It saddened me deeply to think of how long I had been forced to live under such oppression, crushed under its weight with no hope of regaining freedom.

As the bus continued its journey, my attention shifted to the view outside the window. The Serbian countryside stretched out before me, its hills and fields a stark contrast to the oppressive landscapes of my past. But even as the beauty of the present surrounded me, the memory of my father lingered—a reminder of where I had come from and why I had fought so hard to leave.

In that moment, the ache of loss mixed with a glimmer of hope. I had escaped the regime that had taken so much from me, but its shadow remained, shaping the man I had become. As the bus rolled on, I resolved to honor my father's resilience and to find the freedom and peace he had been denied.

Chapter 22

Belgrade

The hours melted away as the bus hummed steadily along, carrying me through the heart of Serbia. Outside the window, the landscapes unfolded like a living painting, each scene more captivating than the last. The rolling hills, dotted with quaint villages and vast stretches of open fields, seemed to hold secrets of a world so different from the one I had known. As we traveled deeper into the country, I found myself marveling at the sheer beauty of this place, a land I had never imagined would leave such an impression on me.

Three hours into the journey, we approached the city of Jagodina, its presence on the horizon hinting at stories untold. The rhythmic motion of the bus and the gentle hum of the engine lulled me into a state of reverie. Each passing moment allowed me to immerse myself in the unfamiliar sights and sounds of a new land, far removed from the familiarity of my Albanian village.

Here I was, traversing unknown territory, experiencing a world I had only dreamed of. The intensity of the moment filled me with wonder and exhilaration. Every landmark, every turn in the road, sparked a sense of curiosity and excitement within me. For a fleeting moment, I forgot the challenges I had faced and allowed myself to revel in the joy of discovery.

As I gazed out at the ever-changing vistas, a pang of longing stirred within me. I thought of my mother and how much I yearned to share this extraordinary journey with her. I imagined her expression as I recounted the details—the vibrant fields, the bustling towns, and the sense of freedom that came with being on the move. Yet, even as I entertained this wish, the harsh reality of our circumstances loomed over me. The distance between us felt insurmountable, and the prospect of ever returning home seemed increasingly remote.

My thoughts shifted, and my father entered my mind, his presence both a source of comfort and sorrow. He was a man of contradictions: intelligent, loving, yet deeply flawed by his struggles with alcoholism. Despite his demons, he was a figure I admired—a man who had achieved so much against the odds. After his brother's death in World War II, my father had done something remarkable for a man from our small, rural village. He pursued an education, even attending veterinary school, a path that set him apart from the others.

Navigating life under the communist regime was no easy feat, and while my father complied with its demands to a degree, he was never truly one of them. He maintained a delicate balance, leveraging his connections to resolve issues without betraying his principles. In a system where dissent could lead to imprisonment or worse, my father's ability to walk this line ensured our family's survival.

From him, I learned lessons that have stayed with me. Chief among them was the value of honesty. My father often told me, *"If you tell the truth, you'll never have to remember anything. You won't have to pretend to be someone you're not."* Yet, even this principle had its limits in a world where truth could be a dangerous weapon. He warned me about speaking openly against the communist system, where a single word out of place could lead to dire consequences. Still, in all other matters, my father held truth as sacred.

Another defining trait of my father was his unyielding belief in education. In a village where most children stopped schooling after the eighth grade, he was a pioneer. All my brothers attended high school, and many went on to college—an extraordinary accomplishment in our community. My father's mantra, repeated often, was simple: *"Education, education, education."* He believed that knowledge was the key to a better life, a shield against the oppressive forces of the regime.

For most of my brothers, his vision became reality. For me, however, it felt like an unreachable dream. Sadness enveloped me as I thought of the opportunities I had lost. Suspended from school indefinitely and cast out by the system, I was left with no future in the Albanian communist regime. It was one of the most devastating blows of my life, and it planted the seeds of my eventual escape. With nothing to lose, I resolved to leave behind the stagnation and oppression that had defined my existence.

The communist government, for all its rhetoric about equality and support, was anything but benevolent. It thrived on corruption, fear, and exploitation, leaving those like me to fend for themselves. My father understood this reality all too well, and though he could not change the system, he tried to shield us from its worst effects.

Thinking of him now, I felt a deep ache of sadness. Despite his flaws, he had been a kind and generous man, doing what he could to guide us through a harsh and unforgiving world. His struggles with alcohol were his way of coping, but even in his darkest moments, he remained my father—a man who had taught me the importance of truth, resilience, and the pursuit of knowledge.

The bus jolted slightly, pulling me from my thoughts. As we neared Belgrade, a sense of determination took hold of me. I resolved to write to my father and mother as soon as I could, if circumstances permitted. The thought of sharing my experiences with them brought a glimmer of comfort amidst the uncertainty of the journey. Perhaps my father's wisdom, the lessons he had instilled in me, would guide me through this unfamiliar land, just as they had shaped my spirit back home.

The bus rumbled on, but my thoughts drifted backward, entangling me in memories of stories my father used to tell about the old days in Albania. One story stood out—a tale that perfectly captured the corrupt and hypocritical nature of the Communist regime.

My father worked as a bartender in those days, a position that placed him at the crossroads of the local community and the powerful elite. One of his regulars was Dino, a vice secretary of the Communist Party. Dino was a large man, tipping the scales at over 300 pounds, with a protruding belly that he carried like a badge of honor. In Albania, such a physique was a mark of wealth and access, a signal that he lived a life of privilege while the rest of us struggled to make ends meet.

Dino would swagger into the tavern daily, ordering food and drinks with an air of entitlement. He always paid with absurdly large bills—500 Albanian Lek for a tab that cost mere cents. My father didn't have the small denominations needed to make change, so Dino would leave without paying, day after day, assuming the tab would vanish like so many of his other privileges.

But my father, meticulous and principled, kept a log of every transaction. He recorded each meal, each drink, and each unpaid tab in a small notebook, silently biding his time. Then one day, Dino returned, flashing his typical 500 Lek bill. This time, my father saw his opportunity. He took the bill and applied it toward Dino's outstanding balance, settling the account in full.

Dino was enraged. His face turned red, his voice booming as he threatened my father. "I'll destroy you as a human being," he roared. For a man like Dino, who thrived on unchecked power and entitlement, being held accountable—even in such a small way—was an affront he couldn't tolerate.

This was the nature of the Communist elite. They preached moral purity, claiming that their system was free from theft, greed, and exploitation. But their words were nothing more than propaganda, hollow slogans designed to maintain control. They lived lives of excess and indulgence, while the common people struggled to survive.

Dino's story wasn't unique. The Communists operated like a well-organized mafia. It was understood—unstated but clear—that to survive, you had to comply. You had to give them what they wanted, no matter how unreasonable, or risk their wrath. If anything went wrong, blame flowed downward like water, always landing on the innocent.

The corruption extended beyond individuals like Dino. The system itself was designed to consolidate power. Communist officials were deliberately sent to govern regions where they had no roots—foreigners ruling over strangers. This ensured loyalty to the party rather than to the local community. By rotating leaders and placing them in unfamiliar territories, the regime severed any ties that might foster dissent or challenge their authority.

These outsiders, loyal to the party and unconnected to the people they governed, carried out the regime's agenda with ruthless efficiency. Their allegiance was to the leader at the top, and as long as they delivered, they enjoyed unfettered power. They ruled with a double standard: preaching equality by day while indulging in corruption and debauchery by night.

It was sickening. The Communists held themselves above the very laws and principles they forced upon the rest of us. They spoke of morality and unity but lived lives riddled with hypocrisy. They had wives and mistresses, wealth and privilege, all while the people they governed barely scraped by. As I sat on the bus, I could almost hear my father's voice recounting these stories, his tone a mix of frustration and sadness. He had witnessed the regime's corruption firsthand, had been entangled in its web, and had suffered for his honesty and integrity. The thought of Dino's threats, of my father's quiet resistance, made my stomach churn.

I turned my attention to the window, hoping to shake off the bitterness of the memory. The Serbian countryside rolled past, its hills and fields a soothing contrast to the oppressive landscapes of my past. But the story lingered, a stark reminder of the world I had left behind—a world where power corrupted absolutely, where loyalty was a tool of control, and where even the most basic acts of honesty could lead to ruin. The hypocrisy of the Communist regime wasn't just a failing; it was a foundation. It was the system's beating heart, ensuring that those in power remained untouchable while the rest of us bore the burden of their lies. Thinking about it now, even miles away from that world, left a bitter taste in my mouth. It was a chapter of my life I was desperate to close, but its lessons were etched into my soul

As the bus continued its steady progress, we passed through the towns of Svilajnac and Lapovo, each one a fleeting glimpse into the tapestry of Serbian life. These small, yet vibrant communities added depth to my understanding of this unfamiliar land, fueling my curiosity and igniting a spark of hope within my soul.

Despite the isolation and uncertainty that surrounded us, I clung to the resilience of my spirit, buoyed by the promise of discovery that lay ahead. With each passing mile, I embraced the journey with renewed vigor, eager to uncover the secrets that lay hidden amidst the vast expanse of Serbia's breathtaking landscapes.

Chapter 23

The Refugee Camp at Padinska Skela

Padinska Skela was a hive of activity, a place caught in the tide of history as refugees from collapsing regimes sought sanctuary. At the time, it was predominantly filled with Romanians fleeing Nicolae Ceaușescu's crumbling rule. The buses arrived in waves, unloading weary faces. Some stayed, holding onto hope for a fresh start, while others were sent back across the border. Across the Danube, refugees streamed in from Timișoara, a city whose name had become synonymous with revolution. It was a tumultuous period, where survival often hinged on luck and timing.

The camp itself, managed by the United Nations High Commissioner for Refugees (UNHCR), was my first encounter with organized humanitarian aid. For a refugee, life is disorienting—a role you never anticipate, thrust into an existence dictated by survival and resilience. Yet for me, it also became an opportunity for curiosity and learning. Padinska Skela was my first glimpse of a world larger than the confines of my small Albanian village, a world bursting with diverse cultures and behaviors.

The room I was assigned to at Padinska Skela was overcrowded and utilitarian, filled with about 20 bunk beds arranged in rigid rows. Each bed was a basic metal frame, creaking under the slightest movement, accompanied by a small, flat pillow and a thin blanket that barely shielded us from the chill. The walls bore the marks of those who had come before—names and messages etched into the plaster. Many were Albanian, their words offering reassurance to those who followed: *We were here. We endured. You will too.*

Time in the camp was surreal. It stretched endlessly and yet seemed to pass in the blink of an eye. Days were punctuated by the clang of the bell summoning us to meals in the mess hall. In between, I sat on my bunk, observing the cacophony around me. The room was alive with conversations, predominantly in Romanian, their rapid-fire exchanges often punctuated by laughter or heated debate. The noise was both comforting and disorienting, a constant reminder of the lives that intersected in this transient space.

Lying on my bunk, I would stare at the peeling ceiling and let my thoughts wander to the past. These reflections felt different here—detached, as though I were watching my own memories unfold from a safe distance. The pain and longing that had once consumed me were muted, replaced by a quiet acceptance of my circumstances.

One memory that lingered was the story of Dalo, a neighbor and childhood friend from my village. Dalo was a goat herder, a simple man who lived a life of quiet routine. His so-called crime was taking seven blankets left outside a government utility company's facility. Dalo thought they were abandoned and brought them home. When the theft was discovered, panic set in, and he hid the blankets rather than risk returning them.

The betrayal came from within—his own brother reported him to the authorities. This act of treachery was emblematic of life under the communist regime, where loyalty to the state often superseded family bonds. Dalo was arrested and taken to the city of Peshkopi before being brought back to our village for a public trial. These trials, staged under the guise of the "dictatorship of the proletariat," were nothing more than theatrical displays of power. The judges, uneducated elders loyal to the Communist Party, were figureheads parroting the regime's decisions. The verdict was predetermined—Dalo was sentenced to seven years in prison for seven blankets. It wasn't about the theft; it was about fear. The regime needed to make an example of him, to demonstrate that even the smallest act of defiance would not go unpunished.

Dalo's story haunted me. It was a symbol of everything I had fled—a life where individuality was crushed under the weight of oppressive control. His pale defeated figure at the trial remained etched in my mind, a reminder of the price of freedom and the resilience it demanded.

...

Life at Padinska Skela was monotonous yet filled with moments of discovery. The routine was predictable: wake up, eat breakfast, mingle in the mess hall, and return to the room. Guards occasionally called individuals for interviews, providing a brief break in the tedium. Despite the crowded conditions, I managed to find moments of connection and learning.

Most of my fellow refugees were Romanian, and I was eager to learn their language. I discovered surprising similarities between Romanian and Albanian, particularly in modern terms derived from Latin roots. These linguistic parallels sparked a fascination with the interconnectedness of cultures. Despite my youth and inexperience, I adapted well. I smiled, avoided conflict, and made an effort to relate to those around me.

One memorable cultural misstep occurred when I parted ways with a Romanian friend and kissed him on the cheek—a gesture of affection common in Albanian culture. His face turned red with embarrassment, and I quickly realized this wasn't a shared custom. It was a small but poignant lesson in navigating the nuances of a new cultural landscape.

...

The 15 days I spent at Padinska Skela passed in a blur of monotony and reflection. The room, though noisy and crowded, became a place of quiet transformation. I observed, listened, and learned. Each interaction, each story, added a layer to my understanding of the world beyond my village.

On the final day, I was told I would be released to Belgrade, where I was scheduled to visit the U.S. embassy within three days for an interview. The news filled me with both excitement and apprehension. I didn't know what lay ahead, but I felt ready to face it. The experiences at Padinska Skela had already begun to shape me, instilling a resilience and curiosity that would carry me forward.

Padinska Skela was more than a refugee camp; it was a crucible of transformation. It exposed me to the rawness of human experience, the resilience of those who endure, and the complexities of navigating a world far removed from the one I had known. It was a place of waiting, but also of growth. In the crowded room with its etched walls and creaking beds, I began to understand the depth of what it meant to survive, and the strength required to forge a new path. As I left the camp, I carried with me the stories, the lessons, and a growing sense of hope for the journey ahead.

Chapter 24

The Journey Forward

The bus rattled forward, its engine grumbling with every shift in gear, a mechanical protest that seemed to echo my own exhaustion. My seat felt stiff beneath me, the fabric worn thin and scratchy against my legs. The air inside the bus was stifling, a mix of sweat, dust, and stale breath. I couldn't escape the sticky heat clinging to my skin, a heat that only seemed to deepen the ache in my body.

I sat near the window, my bag nestled tightly on my lap. My hands gripped its frayed edges as though it held not just my belongings but the last fragile threads of my identity. Through the gaps in the curtains, I caught fleeting glimpses of the world outside—a world that felt close enough to touch yet utterly foreign.

The road stretched ahead, lined with low, tired buildings. Their paint had long since peeled away, exposing cracks that seemed like scars left by years of neglect. Cyrillic letters adorned the faded signs, their meaning a mystery to me, though their age and wear spoke volumes. Sometimes, small shops appeared, their windows crammed with simple necessities—bread, soda bottles, and cartons of cigarettes. Outside, people lingered, shaded by patched awnings or leaning against crumbling walls. Their faces were weathered, their postures unhurried, as though time had slowed for them but sped up for me.

Each scene stirred a complicated mix of emotions. Part of me wanted to step out, to touch these places and perhaps find a sliver of connection in their ordinariness. But another part of me recoiled, afraid that what I found would only underscore how far I was from anything resembling home.

When the bus reached the Danube River, it slowed as if granting us permission to marvel at the view. The river was immense, its surface shimmering like molten glass under the brutal summer sun. Barges moved lazily along its length; their operators' small figures shaded beneath tarps. The breeze carried faint traces of water and something metallic, a scent that clung to the industrial skyline on the far bank.

I pressed my face closer to the window, shifting the curtain aside. For a moment, the beauty of the river felt like a reprieve, a pause in the relentless forward motion. But as the bridge gave way to the busy streets of Belgrade, the weight of reality settled back on my chest.

The city was a patchwork of motion and sound. Apartment blocks rose in dense clusters, their gray exteriors softened by the bright splashes of laundry hanging from balconies. On the streets below, people moved with purpose—carrying bags, hailing taxis, or weaving through clusters of pedestrians. The sounds were muffled inside the bus but unmistakable: car horns, hurried conversations, the occasional burst of laughter.

Inside the bus, the atmosphere was entirely different. There was no laughter here, no bustling energy. Each of us sat with our thoughts, the silence broken only by the occasional murmur in a mix of languages—Romanian, Serbian, and others I couldn't identify. A child whimpered softly in the row ahead, quickly hushed by a mother whose eyes held the same weary patience I saw in so many others. I looked down at my bag, my fingers unconsciously tracing its edges. It contained everything I had left—some clothes, a notebook, a few photographs. Each item was a piece of my past, a past I wasn't sure I could ever return to. The road narrowed as we neared Košutnjak. The urban sprawl faded into something quieter, greener. Trees lined the streets, their branches forming a canopy that dappled the road with shifting light. The houses here were smaller, their tiled roofs red and sloping. Gardens bloomed with summer flowers—reds, yellows, purples—bursting with a life that felt almost defiant against the heat.

When Hotel Trim came into view, I couldn't help but stare. The building was modest, its white walls glowing faintly in the sunlight. It wasn't imposing, yet it felt like a threshold—a place where my old life ended and something entirely unknown began.

The bus came to a halt with a hiss of brakes, and the driver opened the door. I hesitated for a moment, then stepped into the sweltering heat. The sunlight was blinding after the dim interior, and I had to blink several times before I could take in my surroundings. The guards stood near the entrance, their uniforms crisp, their voices sharp and commanding. They gestured us forward, their instructions curt but clear.

The moment my feet touched the ground, the world seemed to shift. The oppressive heat of the sun bore down, but the sight of the building ahead anchored me. Hotel Trim stood amid the trees; its simple architecture framed by the lush greenery of the surrounding neighborhood. The buzz of cicadas was loud here, filling the still air with their relentless rhythm.

Guards directed us toward the entrance, their voices sharp and commanding. They wore uniforms that seemed too heavy for the weather, yet their movements were brisk and efficient. Their instructions were given in Serbian, their gestures firm and unambiguous for those who didn't understand the words. Inside, the air-conditioning was a welcome reprieve. The lobby was stark and functional, its walls painted in neutral tones. Desks were arranged in neat rows, each manned by an officer surrounded by stacks of forms and papers. The emblem of the UNHCR hung prominently on one wall, a reminder of the system that had brought us here.

We were directed to a waiting area, rows of plastic chairs filled with people who mirrored my own exhaustion and apprehension. Quiet conversations in a mix of languages floated through the space, blending with the soft hum of an overhead fan.

Names were called one by one, and individuals were led into smaller rooms where the processing began. When my name was called, I rose hesitantly, clutching my bag tightly as though it might offer protection.

The officer at the desk barely glanced at me as he gestured for me to sit. His questions came quickly, his Serbian rapid and clipped. I struggled to piece together answers, relying on a mix of broken phrases and gestures. At one point, he asked me to empty my bag. I carefully unpacked its meager contents—a notebook, a few clothes, and a photograph or two. He examined each item with detached efficiency, jotting down notes before returning them to me.

When the questioning was complete, he handed me a small card with a number printed on it. My case number. It felt strange in my hand, both tangible and abstract—a symbol of how my identity had been reduced to data in a system I barely understood. I was directed to another waiting area, smaller and quieter. The air felt heavier here, the weight of uncertainty pressing down on everyone. Strangers sat around me, their faces unreadable but their emotions palpable—fear, resignation, and the faintest flicker of hope.

As I sank into my chair, I allowed myself a moment to breathe. The journey to Hotel Trim had been long and draining, but it was only the beginning. The road ahead was still shrouded in uncertainty, but in that moment, I clung to the belief that this place, however temporary, could be the first step toward something new.

The room I was assigned to was small, barely enough space to accommodate the five bunk beds that lined the walls. It was the first time in this journey that I heard my native language spoken—a wave of familiarity in an otherwise foreign and disorienting experience. All five of my roommates were Albanian, each carrying their own stories of escape, loss, and uncertainty.

To my left was Ben, a tall man in his early 40s from Tirana, the capital city of Albania. Ben had a hollow, gaunt face and a deep, resonant voice that seemed to carry the weight of his experiences. He greeted me warmly, calling me "Ice Master," a nickname that immediately made me feel welcomed. Ben was a musician, someone who had fled Albania like me, seeking a better life.

He often spoke about the girlfriend he had left behind, a woman he clearly adored but feared he would never see again. Ben had been stuck in the hotel for over a year, and the stagnation was wearing on him. His depression was palpable, but he masked it with kindness and humor. Ben had a habit of pinching my cheeks with two fingers—an affectionate gesture common in Albania, a way of showing care and familiarity. Despite his struggles, he was the kind of person who tried to make others feel at ease.

Across the room was Goni, a bodybuilder with a temper. He spent much of his time lifting weights in the makeshift gym at the hotel, his physique intimidating but his demeanor hostile. Goni's bullying nature didn't sit well with me, but I refused to let it affect me. One incident stands out vividly in my memory. A friend had brought me a watermelon, a rare treat, and Goni demanded a share. Frustrated by his attitude, I dropped the watermelon on the floor, smashing it, and declared, "If you can take it from me, I rather break it" It was my way of asserting myself, showing that size didn't dictate power. Despite the tension, our interactions never escalated to physical violence, and I learned to navigate his presence without fear.

On the other side of the room was Sadik, whom everyone affectionately called Dik . He was a short man from Sauk, a village near Tirana, with a big personality that brought lightness to the room. Sadik had a knack for humor, often breaking into song with an exaggerated rendition of Tina Turner's *"What's Love Got to Do with It?"* His playful "oh-oh-oh" noises would echo through the room, drawing laughter from everyone.

Sadik carried his own regrets. As the only male child in his family, he felt the heavy burden of having left his family behind in Albania. He often shared his worries about them, but he never let his fears overshadow his ability to make others smile. His resilience was inspiring, and he became the heart of our little group.

Then there was Arben, a bald, lean man from Peshkopi, a city near my own village. Arben immediately referred to me as his "patriot," a term of endearment and shared identity. He took on a protective role, always looking out for me and ensuring I felt included in the group. While Arben was quieter than the others, his presence was reassuring. He, like the rest of us, was grappling with uncertainty, stuck in limbo with no clear path forward.

When I mentioned that I had an interview scheduled with the U.S. embassy in three days, the disbelief on their faces was evident. They had been waiting for years without any progress, and the idea that something might finally move forward seemed almost too good to be true.

Amid the many faces at Hotel Trim, one stood out—Bash, a young man from Fushë-Krujë. From the moment we met, there was an unspoken connection between us, a bond born from the shared weight of displacement and the quiet recognition of someone navigating the same storm. Bash and I quickly became close, forming a friendship that not only carried us through those tumultuous months but also followed us across the ocean to the United States.

Bash was quiet, dependable, and deeply observant. In a world where chaos and unpredictability reigned, he became a steady presence. He was my age, perhaps a year younger, with a calm demeanor that exuded quiet strength. There was a stability about him that felt rare among refugees like us, caught in the uncertainty of waiting. Serbian girls seemed drawn to him, their bright smiles and lingering glances making him the subject of teasing. "You should try smiling back sometime," I'd say, and he'd chuckle softly, shaking his head with a modest grin.

As the days stretched into weeks, Bash and I grew inseparable. Our bond deepened after we were moved as roommates to an ancillary building—a change that felt both promising and isolating. The move marked the beginning of the end of our time at Hotel Trim, a signal that our departure to the United States was imminent. Yet it also brought an extended limbo, where days blurred into nights, and the weight of waiting pressed harder. In this space of prolonged uncertainty, Bash became not just a friend but a brother.

The ancillary building held its own collection of stories, and one of the most compelling belonged to Liman, our neighbor and occasional companion. Liman was an older gentleman, short in stature, with a quiet, reflective presence. A former schoolteacher, he carried himself with a mix of intellectual curiosity and awkwardness, his mannerisms tinged with a certain melancholy. Liman often shared stories of his father, a victim of Albania's Communist regime, whose death had left an indelible scar on him.

Despite his history, Liman held an inexplicable affinity for Russia. While most of us dreamed of reaching Western countries like the United States, he longed to go to the Soviet Union. To him, it represented an ideal—a bastion of Bolshevik values he believed Albania had abandoned. He once attempted to escape Yugoslavia and reach Russia, but his journey ended in heartbreak. He was caught and returned to the same purgatory we all shared, his failure marking him with a deep bitterness.

Bash, too, carried his own burdens. His escape from Albania through the rugged mountains of Kosovo was fraught with danger. He made it to Belgrade, but his closest friend, who had attempted the same journey, was caught and sent back to Albania. Bash rarely spoke of his friend, but when he did, his voice was heavy with pain and guilt.

Survivor's guilt clung to him like a shadow, following him even in the quietest moments.

Despite this, Bash bore his struggles with dignity, using his sorrow as a reminder of why he needed to keep moving forward. His ability to balance the weight of his grief with the hope for a better future was something I admired deeply.

When Bash and I learned we would be traveling to the United States on the same day, it felt like a weight had been lifted. Knowing our fates were intertwined gave us both a sense of comfort and purpose. We spent our remaining days in Belgrade exploring the city together. The streets, alive with vendors and bustling crowds, felt like a strange juxtaposition to our own uncertainty. We laughed at small jokes, shared quiet reflections, and marveled at the resilience of the city, even as we grappled with the unknowns of our own futures.

Bash had a way of making the bleakest moments feel lighter. His quiet humor and steady companionship offered a sense of normalcy in a surreal time. We spoke often of his escape, the mountains of Kosovo, and the life he hoped to build. His regret for his friend lingered, but it was balanced by a determination to make his journey worth the cost.

Liman, in contrast, seemed weighed down by his past. He often spoke of his mother, whom he had left behind in Albania, his regret etched into every word. He carried that regret with him all the way to the United States, but it never left him. Years later, unable to bear the weight of his memories and disappointments, Liman took his own life. His story, though tragic, remains a stark reminder of the emotional toll displacement can take.

In many ways, Bash was my anchor. He reminded me that, even in the face of overwhelming uncertainty, there was strength to be found in connection. Our friendship wasn't merely a product of shared circumstances; it was a lifeline, forged in the crucible of hardship and hope.

Despite the crowded space and the underlying tension, there was an undeniable sense of comfort in being surrounded by people who spoke my language and shared my culture. The familiarity of their voices and the cadence of Albanian conversations brought a sense of belonging, even though I felt like an outsider in some ways. Coming from a small village where Macedonian was the first language, I had only begun learning Albanian at school when I was ten. My accent and phrasing betrayed my rural roots, and I often felt slightly apart from the others. Still, I could deeply understand their struggles—the longing for home, the weight of displacement, and the fears for an uncertain future.

The room was alive with personalities—a mosaic of kindness, humor, tension, and resilience. Each of us carried burdens that shaped how we interacted with one another, but in that shared space, we also formed a bond of survival. For me, those days at Hotel Trim became a masterclass in human nature, an experience that taught me about others and, perhaps more importantly, about myself. It was a time of both deep uncertainty and profound connection, moments I would carry with me for the rest of my life.

The atmosphere in the hotel extended beyond our small room. In the adjacent rooms, more Albanians resided, each with their own stories of escape and survival. I heard whispers of those who had already made it to the United States. Their names became almost mythical as stories about their new lives circulated.

Another figure who left a strong impression was Zenel, the oldest among us. He had been persecuted and imprisoned by the Communist regime, enduring hardships that most of us could only imagine. Zenel carried himself with a sense of purpose, speaking fervently about his dreams of returning to Albania to see the Communist government toppled.

He envisioned himself standing in front of parliament, declaring Albania free and taking over the presidency. It was a grand, almost fantastical vision, and while we admired his passion, we knew how far-fetched it seemed. Yet, his dreams were a reflection of the hope we all carried—a hope that one day, things would be different, that the lives we left behind could somehow be reclaimed.

Zenel's journey, however, was met with disappointment. He was repeatedly denied resettlement in Western countries, his age and circumstances working against him. I watched him wrestle with that rejection; the pain etched into his face as the realization sank in that his dreams might never materialize.

Chapter 25

Stories of Survival and Pride

Every room in the hotel seemed to be filled with stories—tales of escape, of bravery, and of encounters with the oppressive Communist regime. For many, there was a quiet pride in recounting how they had crossed borders, often under the cover of night, risking everything for a chance at freedom. These stories became a way of connecting with one another, of affirming that we were more than refugees; we were survivors.

We spoke often of revolution, of the possibility of overthrowing the Communist government in Albania. The conversations were filled with speculative strategies, grand plans, and the fervent belief that change was not only possible but imminent. It was a kind of collective dreaming that gave us a sense of purpose, even if the reality was far more complex. In the midst of this community, I found close friends who would become like family. Bash, a kind soul from Fushë-Krujë, became my closest companion. Together, we shared hopes and fears, and our bond grew strong enough to carry us through to the United States.

These friendships, forged in the uncertainty of Hotel Trim, were a testament to the human spirit. Despite the hardships, despite the waiting and the fear of rejection, we found ways to connect, to laugh, and to dream.

The hotel was not just a place to sleep; it was a crucible where our stories, personalities, and ambitions collided. It was a space of contradictions—hope and despair, unity and isolation, laughter and tears. In its crowded halls and shared rooms, we learned not just to survive but to hold on to the idea that a better future might still be possible.

The Serbian language came to me easily, almost naturally. Growing up in my village, I had spoken Old Macedonian until I was ten years old. The dialect in my village was a rich, ancient form of Macedonian that bore strong similarities to Serbian. As a result, when I found myself immersed in Serbian, it took very little time for me to pick up the nuances and become fluent. Even though my initial Macedonian was somewhat antiquated, it provided a solid foundation for adapting to modern Serbian.

Yugoslavia was fascinating in its linguistic diversity. The languages were often grouped under the umbrella term "Serbo-Croatian," reflecting the shared linguistic roots of the region. However, each area had its own distinct flavor—Bosnians, Croatians, and Serbians all spoke with unique dialects and intonations. To my ear, Serbian was the clearest and easiest to understand, with its structured pronunciation and familiar cadence.

Belgrade itself was a revelation. The city's beauty was undeniable, with its grand architecture, bustling streets, and vibrant atmosphere. On weekends, my friend Bash and I would roam the city, exploring its landmarks and meeting new people. Bash, far more sophisticated and confident than I was, often led our adventures. One of our favorite activities was going to the train station to meet girls we had connected with in different settings. While Bash was charming and suave, I was more reserved, but I still enjoyed the energy and excitement of these outings. We spent hours wandering through downtown Belgrade, marveling at the city's blend of historical grandeur and modernity.

The city center was particularly captivating, with its striking buildings, squares, and cultural sites. Though I can no longer recall all their names, I vividly remember the National Assembly building, the Kalemegdan Fortress, and the charming streets that crisscrossed the old city. Belgrade had a soul—a mix of history, resilience, and vibrancy that made it one of the most beautiful places I'd ever seen.

At the time, Yugoslavia was a hybrid of socialism and capitalism, a unique system that seemed to work well. It allowed for both state control and entrepreneurial freedom, creating a balance that was visible in Belgrade's thriving streets. Serbian people were warm and welcoming; I found them easy to get along with. Although nationalism and political tensions were part of the broader narrative, I rarely encountered overt hostility. The only exception was the animosity some Serbians held toward Kosovo Albanians. This tension, while present, didn't dominate my interactions. Instead, I focused on building relationships and navigating life in this new environment.

...

Shortly after arriving at Hotel Trim, I began to establish myself. I found work as a subcontractor, acting as a middleman between Albanian laborers and Serbian employers. I communicated on behalf of the Albanian workers, negotiated their rates, and arranged their jobs. For my services, I took a significant cut—fifty percent of their earnings. Though it might seem exploitative, it was a role that required trust and resourcefulness, and it allowed me to stay occupied and earn a living.

This arrangement introduced me to the day-to-day lives of Serbian people, who hired workers for various tasks. It also gave me insight into the economic system, which was more dynamic than I had expected. Despite the challenges, I learned how to navigate this space, building bridges between communities that didn't always trust each other.

Soon after my arrival, I visited the United Nations building in Belgrade. It was a stark, functional structure, a reminder of the bureaucracy that governed the lives of refugees like me. There, I was issued an identification card called *"Legitimacija"*, which became my lifeline in a foreign land. Along with the ID, they handed me a single-page document that stated my name, origins, and vocation.

At that time, my "vocation" was simply listed as "labor." It was a stark reflection of my circumstances—no past achievements, no future prospects, just the acknowledgment of my ability to work. It felt humbling, even reductive, but it was also a step forward. With that piece of paper, I had a semblance of identity in a system that oftentimes stripped people of their individuality.

Life in Belgrade was a mix of contrasts. On the one hand, there was the joy of discovery—the beauty of the city, the camaraderie of new friendships, and the sense of independence that came from navigating a foreign environment. On the other hand, there was the weight of displacement—the longing for home, the uncertainty of the future, and the challenges of surviving in a world where every step felt like a negotiation.

Through it all, I found ways to adapt and grow. The Serbian language became a tool for connection, opening doors to experiences and relationships I might otherwise have missed. The city, with its complexities and contradictions, became both a challenge and a sanctuary. And amidst the chaos of refugee life, I began to carve out a path that was uniquely my own.

Belgrade, the capital of Serbia, is a city steeped in history and culture, sitting at the confluence of the Sava and Danube rivers. It is one of Europe's oldest cities, with landmarks that reflect its dynamic past and vibrant present. During my time there, I explored its streets and iconic locations, each one leaving a lasting impression. Belgrade was beautiful—an ancient yet vibrant city that unfolded like a storybook with each turn of its streets. My experiences there were a mix of discovery and awe, each place leaving an indelible mark on my memory. The city had a way of captivating the soul, its landmarks not just sights to see but chapters in its living history. Here's how I experienced these unforgettable places.

Kalemegdan Fortress was one of the first places I visited in Belgrade, and it left me awestruck. Perched on a hill where the Sava and Danube rivers meet, the fortress seemed to carry the weight of centuries. Walking through its gates and along its walls, I felt the echoes of history— Roman soldiers, Ottoman rulers, and countless others who had stood where I now stood.

I loved to linger at the edge of the fortress, looking out over the rivers. The view was breathtaking, a reminder of both the city's resilience and the beauty of its natural surroundings. Sometimes, I'd sit on the old stone benches, imagining the lives of those who had defended these walls. Kalemegdan became my refuge, a place where I could feel the pull of history and the peace of nature all at once.

Republic Square was the pulse of the city. Whenever I stood there, surrounded by the grandeur of the National Museum and the National Theatre, I felt like I was in the very heart of Belgrade. The statue of Prince Mihailo on horseback seemed to watch over the bustling square, a symbol of the city's independence and pride. I often found myself there, people-watching and soaking in the energy. The square was always alive with street performers, vendors, and groups of friends chatting under the open sky. It was a place where the past and present collided—a living museum where history breathed alongside modern life.

Knez Mihailova Street was where I truly felt the charm of Belgrade. Its pedestrian-only pathways were lined with elegant shops, quaint cafes, and historic buildings that seemed to whisper stories from a bygone era.

Many a day I often walked along Knez Mihailova, sipping coffee from street-side cafes or window-shopping. The street was always buzzing, yet it had a calmness to it— a space where you could take your time and enjoy the moment. I remember pausing in front of a bookstore once, the smell of fresh coffee mingling with the crisp air, and thinking how this street embodied everything I loved about Belgrade.

Saint Sava Temple left me speechless. Its massive white marble facade and green domes dominated the skyline, but it was the sense of spiritual grandeur that struck me most. Walking into the temple felt like stepping into a sacred space that transcended time. Though the interior was still under construction during my visit, the mosaics and frescoes that adorned its walls were stunning. I remember standing in the center of the unfinished hall, looking up at the golden dome, and feeling an overwhelming sense of awe. It was a place that reminded me of the power of faith and the beauty of human ambition.

Skadarlija was pure magic. Its cobblestone streets and old-world charm transported me to a different era, a place where time seemed to move slower. The street was lined with traditional Serbian restaurants, art galleries, and antique shops, and the air was filled with the sound of live music. I often dined there, sharing with my Serbian friends meals of grilled meats and sipping local wine. One evening, a band played traditional Serbian folk music, and the entire street seemed to come alive. We laughed, ate, and soaked in the atmosphere, feeling connected not just to the city but to its soul.

Ada Ciganlija was a retreat—a slice of nature within the city. Known as Belgrade's "Sea," the river island offered beaches, sports facilities, and plenty of open space to unwind. On sunny days, Many of my Albanian refuge friend and I would head there to relax by the water, watching families picnic and children play. The island had a peaceful energy, a stark contrast to the bustling streets of downtown. One afternoon, we rented bicycles and rode around the island, feeling the breeze on our faces and the sun on our backs. It was freedom, pure and simple.

Zemun felt like stepping into another world. Its cobblestone streets and riverside charm made it feel like a small town, separate from the rest of Belgrade. The Gardoš Tower stood proudly, offering panoramic views of the city and the Danube River. Climbing the tower was a memorable experience for me. From the top, we could see the red-tiled roofs of Zemun's houses and the river stretching into the distance. It was quiet, serene, and utterly captivating—a place where the hustle of Belgrade faded into the background.

The Belgrade Waterfront was unlike anything else in the city. Its sleek, modern design was a testament to the city's ambition and progress. High-rise buildings, luxury apartments, and wide promenades lined the riverbank, creating a space that felt forward-looking and dynamic. Walking along the waterfront, I was struck by how Belgrade managed to balance its rich history with its aspirations for the future. It was a place of possibility, a reminder that the city was always evolving.

I experienced Belgrade through my own eyes, and its essence is a vision I will cherish forever. Each place I visited has unique significance, etched deeply into my memory, becoming an inseparable part of my story.

Chapter 26

The Interview and the Days Leading to Departure

When I finally showed up at the U.S. Embassy for my interview, I wasn't sure what to expect. My friend Bash was called in as well, and we went together, both anxious and uncertain about what lay ahead. Stories of others being denied entry to the United States had circulated widely among refugees, and the possibility of rejection loomed large in my mind. I tried to prepare myself for any outcome, even considering that I might need to apply to another country like Germany or Australia if things didn't work out.

The interview itself was straightforward, yet it left me unsettled. The questions were simple—who I was, how old I was, and whether I had committed any crimes. I don't recall the exact details of the conversation, but I do remember the tension in the air, the weight of knowing that my future hinged on the outcome. Despite the simplicity of the questions, it wasn't an easy interview to give.

A few days later, the news came: the United States had accepted my application for refuge. I would be going to a place called Boise, Idaho. I had never heard of Boise before, nor could I imagine what awaited me there. The plan was to fly to New York first and then take another flight westward to Idaho. The names of these places felt foreign, abstract, like destinations on a map I had yet to understand.

Although I had learned English in school back in Albania and could speak it relatively well, I knew that communicating in a new country would still be a challenge. There was much to learn—not just the language, but the culture, the way people lived and worked, and how I would fit into this new world. The excitement of starting over was mixed with the fear of the unknown. In the days leading up to my departure, I wandered the city, spending my time drinking and reflecting. One memory stands out, a mix of humor and absurdity that has stayed with me.

During this time, I was at Hotel Yugoslavia in Novi Beograd and working as a laborer for a contractor.

My job was to remodel rooms alongside a small group of workers I had brought together. One afternoon, I went out to get food for lunch. I stopped at a small store, where I ended up sitting with a group of Serbian men.

They were unmistakably drunk, their voices slurred as they lamented the state of the nation and grumbled about the Kosovars. I joined them, snacking on salami and slices of delicious Serbian French bread while washing it all down with several beers. The conversation flowed in a mix of grumbles and laughter, but I wasn't paying much attention—I was just soaking in the moment, enjoying the food and the company.

By the time I returned to the worksite, I had more than a few beers in me. I brought the food back to my crew and then headed off to take a shower, trying to shake off the haze of the afternoon. But when I came out of the shower, it was clear to everyone that I was drunk. My friend Bash looked at me with a mix of amusement and disbelief, jokingly declaring, "You got drunk in the shower!"

We laughed about it later, and while it wasn't my proudest moment, it became one of those stories that we retold, a bit of levity during a time that was otherwise filled with uncertainty.

...

As my departure drew closer, I felt a mixture of emotions. There was relief at being accepted by the United States, gratitude for the opportunity, and a growing curiosity about what life in Boise, Idaho, would be like. At

146

the same time, there was sadness at leaving behind the familiar—even the flawed and difficult circumstances I had grown used to in Belgrade.

The transition was imminent, and I knew that the experiences and lessons I had gathered during my time in Serbia would shape the way I approached the next chapter of my life. Whether it was navigating a tense interview, adapting to a foreign culture, or simply learning how to laugh at myself, these moments had prepared me for the unknown. Boise was waiting, and with it, a new beginning.

Time flew by, and before I knew it, my trip was scheduled for November 3rd, 1988. Those six months in Belgrade had passed in a haze of learning, adaptation, and self-discovery. In truth, much of it was fueled by alcohol. Almost every day, I drank—Serbia's mild beers became both a companion and a distraction. The alcohol dulled my memories, helping me detach from the weight of my past, my family, and the place I had come from. It was as if I had stepped into an entirely new reality, one where curiosity and the thrill of the present overshadowed the burdens of yesterday.

The beers were light and left no headaches the next day, allowing me to indulge without consequence. In those months, I blended seamlessly into Serbian life. The language, the culture, and even the rhythm of the people felt natural to me. By the end of my stay, I felt like I belonged, as though I had carved out a small space for myself in this vibrant and complicated world.

Chapter 27

A Writer's Transformation

As a child growing up in the rugged landscapes of Albania, writing was my sanctuary. It was more than just a pastime; it was a lifeline to a world beyond the confines of my small village. My pen became a tool of liberation, crafting stories that soared beyond the mountains that hemmed us in. In the pages of my imagination, I built vast, intricate worlds, populated by characters who defied the limitations of our reality. Writing wasn't just something I did, it was who I was. I dreamt of one day creating a book that would transcend boundaries, a masterpiece brimming with vivid imagery and profound insights, a bridge between the tangible and the abstract.

But now, in Belgrade, that dream felt like a distant echo of another life. My journey had been one of survival, adaptation, and transformation, and in the whirlwind of change, my identity as a writer seemed to slip further away. I was no longer the boy who wrote by candlelight in a quiet Albanian village. Immersed in the dynamic, unfamiliar rhythms of a new city and a new language, I found myself untethered, struggling to hold onto the essence of who I had been.

Serbian was no longer just a language I heard—it had begun to infiltrate my thoughts, my dreams, and even my way of understanding the world. My mind, once a canvas painted with the words and imagery of my native tongue, now felt like a puzzle of two languages interlocking and at times colliding. Each day brought new phrases, expressions, and ways of thinking, reshaping how I perceived my surroundings and myself. It was both exhilarating and unsettling, this evolution of thought and identity. I often wondered what this transformation meant for my dream of becoming a writer. Writing had always been the purest expression of my inner self, yet now my words felt foreign, caught between two worlds. How could I reconcile the rich, lyrical depth of my Albanian roots with the emerging structures of Serbian, and eventually, the vast ocean of possibilities within English? Would I ever again find the clarity and confidence to create something truly meaningful?

In some ways, the transition was a gift. Each new word, each cultural nuance I absorbed in Belgrade, added layers to my understanding of the world. I cherished the experiences and memories I was collecting—the sound of the Danube's waters brushing against its banks, the bustling markets filled with chatter, and the fleeting kindness of strangers in a foreign land. These moments were rich with inspiration, the lifeblood of any writer's craft. And yet, I mourned the loss of simplicity—the ease with which my thoughts once flowed, unimpeded by the complexities of translation and adaptation.

The process of redefining my voice felt like wandering through a dense forest without a map. I stumbled, faltered, and at times, wanted to abandon the journey altogether. But deep within, I knew this transformation held the seeds of something profound. To think and dream in multiple languages was to see the world through different lenses, each offering its own truths and perspectives. Perhaps the writer I was becoming would not be limited by a single identity but enriched by the collision of many.

I began to envision my future in an English-speaking country, where yet another linguistic and cultural transformation awaited. Would my voice emerge stronger, tempered by the trials of adaptation, or would I lose myself further in the shifting sands of identity? The question loomed over me, unanswered, but not unwelcome. It was a challenge, a call to stretch the boundaries of my creativity and resilience.

In the quiet moments, I reminded myself of the purpose that had always driven me: the desire to connect. To build bridges between the seen and unseen, the spoken and unspoken. Perhaps my path as a writer would never be straightforward, but then again, the most compelling stories are rarely without twists and turns. My transformation, though disorienting, was a story in itself—one that I had yet to fully understand but knew would shape the pages I would one day write.

The dream of a boy in Albania hadn't disappeared; it was evolving. It wasn't just about writing a book anymore. It was about embracing the richness of change, weaving the threads of my past, present, and future into something that could speak to the complexity of human experience. My voice, though uncertain now, would find its way. And when it did, it would carry within it the echoes of every word, every language, and every transformation that had brought me here.

Despite the challenges, I developed a deep appreciation for Serbian culture. The people I met were kind and genuine, their hospitality a stark contrast to the stereotypes I had heard before arriving. While history painted Serbians as aggressors and ethnic cleansers, my experience told a different story. The Serbians I knew were deeply connected to one another and to their faith. Their Orthodox religion gave them a sense of purpose and community that I found admirable. They cared for one another in a way that felt profound and sincere, and I was welcomed with open hearts. I often marveled at their resilience and their ability to find joy and meaning in daily life. I make no secret of it—I loved Serbian culture. It was rich and meaningful, rooted in traditions that resonated deeply with me. Yet, I also understood that history is tainted by bias and the weight of political narratives. The kindness I experienced did not erase the complexities of the nation's past or its future.

Chapter 28

Politics, Nationalism, and the Path to War

Even as I cherished my time in Serbia, I could feel the undercurrents of something darker—a tide of politics and nationalism that would soon engulf the nation. The landscape of Yugoslavia in late 1988 was shifting, and its fragility was becoming apparent.

The rise of **Slobodan Milošević** was a pivotal moment in this transformation. By November 1988, Milošević was solidifying his power, having positioned himself as a champion of Serbian nationalism. His speeches resonated with a growing sense of discontent among Serbs, especially in Kosovo, where tensions with the Albanian population were boiling over. Milošević's rhetoric, filled with promises to protect Serbian interests, struck a chord with many who felt marginalized in the multi-ethnic framework of Yugoslavia.

At the time, Milošević had already begun centralizing power, dismantling the autonomy of provinces like Kosovo and Vojvodina. This was a direct challenge to the federal structure of Yugoslavia, where power was meant to be balanced among its six republics and two autonomous provinces. His actions stirred anxiety among the other republics, particularly Croatia and Slovenia, which viewed his moves as a threat to their sovereignty.

The nationalism he fueled wasn't confined to political speeches—it seeped into everyday life. While much of Serbia seemed at peace, you could hear murmurs of dissatisfaction in conversations at cafes or marketplaces. People spoke with a mix of pride and unease about Serbia's place in Yugoslavia, often blaming "the others" for perceived grievances.

The Yugoslavia I knew was a beautiful mosaic of cultures and religions, a place where diversity was celebrated in theory. Yet, beneath this harmony, deep-seated tribalism, territorial disputes, and political ambitions were being manipulated. The leadership—driven by pecuniary and political interests—exploited these divides for their gain, wrapping their agendas in the guise of ethnic and religious conflicts.

By the end of 1988, it was clear that Yugoslavia was headed toward an uncertain future. Protests, strikes, and a growing sense of distrust between the republics painted a grim picture. In Belgrade, I heard debates among locals about whether Yugoslavia could survive as a unified state. Many clung to hope, but the seeds of division had already been planted.

I didn't believe the wars that later consumed Yugoslavia were truly about religion or culture. The people I met were too connected, too genuine to be divided by such things alone. These were conflicts born of economic and political ambitions, cloaked in nationalist rhetoric that stoked fear and hatred. For me, as a refugee looking for a new beginning, this political turmoil added an extra layer of urgency to my journey. I had escaped one oppressive regime in Albania, and now, as I witnessed the unraveling of Yugoslavia, I realized how fragile peace and unity could be. The rise of Milošević and the growing nationalism in Serbia were harbingers of the storm that would soon engulf the region, forever altering the lives of those who called it home.

Chapter 29

A City That Left Its Mark

As I prepared to leave Belgrade, I reflected on all I had learned and experienced. The city had changed me. It had opened my eyes to the complexities of human nature, the beauty of connection, and the destructive power of political manipulation.

Belgrade was not just a place I passed through; it was a chapter in my life that shaped who I was becoming. It was where I learned to adapt, to see beyond stereotypes, and to embrace the richness of a culture different from my own. Even as I boarded the plane for my new life in Boise, Idaho, I carried a part of Belgrade with me—a city of beauty, complexity, and resilience that would forever remain in my heart.

The Journey Begins: November 3rd, 1988

On the morning of November 3rd, 1988, I was picked up alongside my friend Bash and a few other Albanians to be taken to the airport in Belgrade. It was a part of the city I had never seen before, and I had no idea what awaited me. The thought of flying was foreign, something I had only seen on television. I had never been on a plane before, and the entire experience felt distant, surreal, and beyond my understanding.

The flight was with Pan Am, departing from Belgrade with a brief stop in Zagreb, Croatia. From there, it would cross Scotland and Great Britain before reaching New York City's John F. Kennedy Airport. As I absorbed this information, the names of these places—Zagreb, Scotland, New York—felt like words from another world. They were places I'd only heard about in passing, locations that carried no tangible meaning in my mind.

Despite the unfamiliarity, I wasn't worried. I had heard stories about the United States—tales of a better life, a place where opportunities were abundant, and dreams could come true. Somehow, amidst the apprehension and the unknown, there was a flicker of excitement. This was the moment I had imagined so many times, the culmination of fantasies about a land I had never seen but hoped would hold a brighter future.

As I stood at the airport, watching planes land and take off, I was filled with a mix of curiosity and disbelief. These massive chunks of metal, roaring down the runway and soaring into the sky, defied everything I understood about the world. I remember thinking, *How is this even possible?* I laughed to myself, imagining them as "big donkeys flying," a phrase that seemed fitting in its absurdity.

When it was finally time to board the plane, I felt a knot of fear tighten in my chest. I had no frame of reference for what to expect. My only knowledge of airplanes came from movies or vague descriptions, and none of it prepared me for the sensation of flight. As the plane began to taxi down the runway, a sense of unease gripped me. The idea of this massive machine lifting off the ground with so many souls on board felt unnatural. Yet, as I looked around, I saw people smiling, chatting, and settling into their seats with calmness. Their confidence gave me hope. If they trusted this journey, perhaps I could too.

Once the plane lifted into the air, my fear gave way to wonder. I had a window seat in the middle of the plane, and I spent the entire flight glued to the view outside. The clouds looked like endless bundles of cotton, drifting effortlessly through the sky. It was mesmerizing, almost magical, to see the world from above—a perspective I had never imagined.

In the distance, I spotted another plane, its white contrail cutting through the blue expanse of the sky. The sight took me back to my village, where my father would watch planes fly overhead. In Albania, he used to point to the streaks in the sky and tell me they were postal planes, carrying letters or packages. We had no real understanding of air travel in our small, isolated world behind the Iron Curtain. In those days, the world beyond our borders felt like a faraway myth, shrouded in mystery and unreachable.

As I gazed out of the window, I felt the enormity of the moment. This wasn't just a journey to a new place; it was the start of a new life. Everything I had known was behind me, and everything ahead was a mystery. The clouds seemed to symbolize the in-between—the space where I was neither here nor there, suspended between my past and my future.

The memories of my father's voice, the stories of my village, and the dreams I held for the United States swirled in my mind. This was more than a flight; it was a transformation. For the first time, I was stepping out into the world, leaving behind the isolation of Albania and entering a global stage. The thought of landing in New York City, a place I could barely comprehend, filled me with both fear and excitement. I didn't know what to expect, but I carried with me a sense of hope—a belief that this journey, strange and daunting as it was, would lead to something better.

In that moment, as the plane soared above the clouds, I felt small yet connected to something much larger. The world was opening before me, and I was ready to embrace it, one uncertain step at a time.

Once the initial thrill of takeoff settled, the flight became an entirely new experience—a mix of awe, introspection, and the slow passing of time. It was my first long journey in the air, and every detail felt significant, like it was part of a story I would retell for years to come.

The hum of the engines became a constant, almost soothing backdrop as the plane leveled out above the clouds. I adjusted in my seat, trying to make sense of the strange sensation of floating high above the earth. The seatbelt sign turned off, and passengers began to move about. The flight attendants walked the aisles with calm efficiency, their uniforms crisp and professional. They offered drinks and small snacks, which I hesitated to accept at first, unsure of the etiquette.

Bash, sitting a few rows behind me, caught my eye and smiled. He gave me a small wave, and I felt reassured knowing he was there. Around me, people settled into conversations, reading books, or leaning back to rest. Some even seemed to sleep, which I couldn't imagine doing I was too restless, too captivated by the novelty of it all.

Not long into the flight, the attendants began serving meals. I had no idea what to expect, and when the tray was placed in front of me, I stared at it with curiosity. It contained a neatly packaged assortment: a warm entrée, a small salad, a piece of bread, and a tiny dessert. The food was different from anything I had eaten before, but I was eager to try it.

The meal felt like an event, breaking up the monotony of sitting still for hours. As I ate, I listened to the quiet hum of conversations around me, catching snippets of different languages—English, Serbian, and others I couldn't identify. The diversity on the plane was remarkable, and it made me realize just how far I was stepping from the world I had known.

My eyes kept drifting to the window. The landscape below was hidden by the thick carpet of clouds, but occasionally, there were breaks where I could see glimpses of land—patchworks of fields, rivers, and clusters of towns. The vastness of it all struck me. I thought about how small my village had seemed in comparison, nestled in the mountains of Albania, so isolated from the rest of the world.

The clouds themselves became a source of fascination. They looked soft and weightless, like giant pillows floating in the sky. At times, the sunlight would pierce through them, creating streaks of gold that lit up the endless blue horizon. I watched another plane pass by in the distance, its contrail cutting across the sky like a line drawn by a child's hand. It was hard to believe that, up here, we were all part of this immense, interconnected world.

As the hours passed, I began to strike up small conversations with the people around me. My English wasn't perfect, but it was good enough to get by. The passengers were friendly, asking me where I was headed and sharing their own stories of travel. Some were Americans returning home; others were Europeans visiting family or friends.

One older man beside me spoke in broken English about his life in Scotland and his travels across Europe. His kindness made me feel at ease, and we exchanged simple stories. He seemed curious about my background, and I explained, in bits and pieces, that I was heading to the United States for the first time. He nodded and said, "You'll do well there. It's a good place to start over."

Despite the excitement, eight hours on a plane felt long. The novelty of the flight eventually gave way to restlessness. I shifted in my seat, stretched my legs, and leaned against the window, staring into the endless sky. The noise of the engines became a kind of white noise, and I felt myself drifting between daydreams and brief moments of sleep.

At one point, I imagined what New York City would be like. All I knew of it came from vague descriptions and stories—skyscrapers, busy streets, and a city that never slept. It was hard to fathom such a place, and harder still to imagine that I was on my way there.

When the plane reached the Atlantic, the realization hit me: I was leaving Europe behind. The water below was vast and endless, a dark expanse that seemed to stretch forever. There were no landmarks, no signs of life— just the plane and the open sky.

It was humbling to think about how far I was traveling. The sheer distance between my past and the future ahead of me felt enormous, both literally and figuratively. I couldn't help but wonder what my family would think if they could see me now, flying over an ocean, headed to a place none of us could have imagined.

As the flight neared its end, the mood on the plane shifted. People began to stir, checking their belongings and straightening their seats. The captain announced our descent into New York, and my heart raced. The thought of landing in the United States, a country I had heard so much about but never truly understood, filled me with anticipation.

Looking out the window, I caught my first glimpse of American soil—tiny dots of light that grew brighter and more numerous as we approached. The city below looked like a sea of stars, stretching as far as the eye could see. It was beautiful, overwhelming, and utterly foreign.

Chapter 30

Touchdown: The Threshold of a New Dawn

The plane's wheels struck the runway at Kennedy Airport with a jarring finality, as if punctuating the long sentence of my journey. In that instant, the turbulence of my past—the pain, the fear, the sacrifices—seemed to dissolve into the background, leaving only the clarity of the present. The flight was over. But as the engines roared their conclusion, a question hummed in my chest: *What comes next?*

I scanned the faces of my fellow passengers. Each person had arrived with their own burdens, dreams, and untold stories. Some stared blankly ahead, still lost in their thoughts, while others smiled at the thought of reunions awaiting them. Yet, for me, this wasn't just the end of a flight—it was the beginning of something far greater. For eight hours, the quiet hum of the aircraft had been a cocoon for my thoughts, a place to reflect on the life I had left and to dream of the life ahead. But now, with the ground beneath me, those dreams faced reality. The future awaited, vivid and uncharted, shimmering on the horizon like a mirage I couldn't yet reach.

Stepping off the plane at Kennedy Airport, the enormity of the moment struck me like a sudden storm. The terminal, vast and bustling, seemed alive with energy, its high ceilings arching above polished floors that stretched endlessly. Outside, the sleek, modern buildings of glass, steel, and concrete stood against a backdrop of highways crowded with honking taxis and shuttles. Through the towering windows, I glimpsed the tarmac, where planes from all over the world lined up, their tails bearing vibrant logos—a testament to the global crossroads that is New York.

Inside, the air buzzed with the sounds of life and motion: luggage wheels rolling, announcements blaring in multiple languages, and conversations blending into a low hum. The terminal was a swirl of activity, with long lines at check-in counters and security gates, overhead signs flashing directions in bold colors. Families reunited with laughter and tears, while travelers rushed to catch connecting flights. Shops filled with everything from snacks to luxury goods lined the pathways, their brightly lit displays offering momentary distractions. The smell of coffee and fast food wafted through the air, mingling with the faint tang of jet fuel.

As I walked deeper into the terminal, the energy around me felt almost overwhelming, yet I spotted them quickly—a small group holding a sign with my name carefully scrawled across it. Strangers from the World Church Service, they stood with warm smiles and welcoming eyes, their presence a lifeline in the swirling chaos. They were my first connection to this new world, a bridge between the life I had left behind and the unknown stretching endlessly before me. Their kindness, though simple, felt monumental.

Yet, as I approached them, the weight of my journey became unbearable. The years of hardship, the sacrifices, the losses—all of it surged forward in an uncontrollable tide. Before I could stop myself, my knees buckled, and I fell to the ground, right there in the bustling terminal. Time seemed to pause. Around me, the world continued to move—a blur of hurried footsteps, rolling suitcases, and fragmented voices—but I was trapped in a moment of suspended reality. I was no longer the person I had been, yet I was not fully the person I would become. I was caught between two worlds: the past I couldn't quite leave behind and the future I didn't yet know how to face.

Memories flooded me—vivid and relentless. I saw my village, nestled among rolling hills and golden fields, where life had once seemed so simple and full of possibility. The faces of my family, etched with love and worry, flashed before me like scenes from an old film. I remembered the years of struggle, the nights spent wondering if this moment would ever come, and the flickering hope that had kept me moving forward. Each memory struck like a wave, pulling me under, until I could no longer hold back the tears.

But beneath the grief and exhaustion, something else began to rise. A quiet, unshakable truth: *I am free.*

Freedom, I realized in that moment, was far more complicated than I had imagined. It wasn't just the absence of chains or the end of oppression—it was a double-edged sword, exhilarating and terrifying in equal measure. With the chains of the past broken, I was untethered, navigating a world with no map and no anchor. The freedom I had longed for, fought for, was now mine, but it came with a weight I hadn't anticipated.

Slowly, I rose to my feet. My legs trembled under the weight of the moment, but with each step, I felt a growing strength, a quiet resolve. Around me, the airport buzzed with life, a reminder that the world was vast and full of potential. The air felt different here—charged with possibility, alive with hope.

I was no longer the person who had boarded that plane. That version of me—the one weighed down by fear and doubt—had been left behind somewhere over the ocean. Yet, I wasn't fully the person I would become. In this in-between, this chrysalis of transformation, one truth shone: *I had crossed a threshold.* This was more than an arrival—it was a rebirth. My journey wasn't defined by what I had escaped, but by the freedom I had claimed. The past would always be a part of me, a foundation for the new life I was about to build.

As I took my first steps into this unfamiliar world, a surge of fierce, unrelenting hope erupted within me, consuming every doubt and fear. It wasn't fragile or fleeting—it was unyielding, a force as steadfast as the roots of a mighty tree anchoring me to this moment. Tears blurred my vision, but the storm of emotions within me raged louder. Then, in a single, breathtaking instant, it hit me: *This was my flight to freedom.*

Geographic Context

To give readers a clearer understanding of the area where my story takes place, I've included references to its geographical location. The journey unfolds across several countries in the Balkans—Albania, Serbia, and Macedonia—regions rich in history and diversity.

Albania is located in southeastern Europe, bordered by Greece to the south, North Macedonia to the east, Kosovo to the northeast, and Montenegro to the northwest. To the west, across the Adriatic Sea, lies Italy. This positioning places Albania at the crossroads of southern Europe, making it a melting pot of cultures and histories over centuries.

Macedonia (now North Macedonia), nestled to the east of Albania, has long shared cultural and historical ties with Albania. To the north lies Serbia, where much of my story takes place after I crossed the border. This intricate patchwork of countries creates a vibrant yet tumultuous setting for my journey.

The Village of Klenje, Albania

The village of Klenje, my birthplace, is located near the eastern border of Albania, close to the Macedonian frontier. Surrounded by rugged, mountainous terrain, Klenje offers a glimpse into the rural life of Albania during the communist era. Its remote location, cradled by the Golemo Mountain, shaped my early years with its harsh winters and modest living conditions.

There are, interestingly, three places named Klenje in the region—one in North Macedonia, another in Serbia, and the one I call home in Albania. The Albanian Klenje stands out as a small, close-knit village where tradition and hardship intertwined, a stark contrast to the cities I would later encounter in my journey.

The Journey: From Klenje to Belgrade

The path from Klenje to Belgrade is both literal and symbolic. My journey began in the mountainous outskirts of Albania, traversing through Macedonia and eventually crossing into Serbia. Each step of the way represented a challenge: crossing borders guarded with vigilance, navigating unfamiliar terrains, and leaving behind the only life I had ever known.

From Klenje, the route eastward would have taken me through the rugged landscapes of eastern Albania, past border towns like Pogradec or Korçë, and into Macedonia. In Macedonia, I likely passed through the city of Struga or

Ohrid, near the iconic Lake Ohrid, before heading north toward Serbia.

In Serbia, the capital city of Belgrade became a pivotal stop in my journey. Located at the confluence of the Sava and Danube Rivers, Belgrade was vastly different from the small village of Klenje. Its grand architecture, bustling streets, and imposing landmarks made it both intimidating and awe-inspiring. It was here that my journey took on new dimensions, with the promise of freedom tantalizingly close yet fraught with uncertainties.

Visualizing the Region

For a better perspective, I've included a Google Maps reference that highlights the region's key locations—Klenje in Albania, the surrounding Balkan countries, and the journey to Belgrade. This visual aid will help contextualize the physical journey and the obstacles I faced in escaping the confines of communism.

Reflections

This area of the world, so rich in history and complexity, serves as both the backdrop and a character in my story. The intertwining of mountains, rivers, and borders creates a landscape as challenging as the struggles of those who navigate it. My path from Klenje to Belgrade was more than just a route; it was a testament to resilience, courage, and the hope for a better future.

www.ingramcontent.com/pod-product-compliance
Lightning Source LLC
Chambersburg PA
CBHW071220090426
42736CB00014B/2911